HOW TO BE A
Maths
Whizz

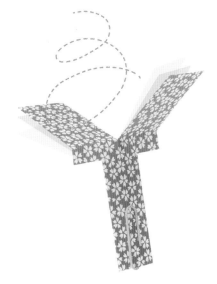

Written by
Dr. Anne-Marie Imafidon

DK | Penguin Random House

Written by Dr. Anne-Marie Imafidon
Consultants Sean McArdle, Meryl Glicksman

Editors Sally Beets, Kathleen Teece
Senior designers Katie Knutton, Ann Cannings
Additional editorial Katie Lawrence, Abigail Luscombe
Design assistants Eleanor Bates, Katherine Marriott
Additional design Emma Hobson, Aishwariya Chattoraj, Nidhi Mehra
Illustrations Mark Ruffle, Katie Knutton
DTP designer Nityanand Kumar
Project picture researcher Sakshi Saluja
Publishing manager Francesca Young
Jacket co-ordinator Issy Walsh
Jacket designer Katie Knutton
Managing editors Laura Gilbert, Jonathan Melmoth
Managing art editor Diane Peyton Jones
Pre-production producer Dragana Puvacic
Senior producer Ena Matagic
Creative directors Clare Baggely, Helen Senior
Publishing director Sarah Larter

First published in Great Britain in 2020 by
Dorling Kindersley Limited
DK, One Embassy Gardens, 8 Viaduct Gardens,
London, SW11 7BW

The authorised representative in the EEA is
Dorling Kindersley Verlag GmbH. Arnulfstr. 124,
80636 Munich, Germany

A CIP catalogue record for this book
is available from the British Library.
ISBN: 978-0-2415-4404-4

Printed and bound in China

For the curious
www.dk.com

This book was made with Forest Stewardship Council™ certified paper – one small step in DK's commitment to a sustainable future. For more information go to www.dk.com/our-green-pledge

Contents

4 Foreword by Dr. Anne-Marie Imafidon
6 How this book works
8 Getting ready

1 Edible maths

12 Counting
14 Edible abacus
16 Watermelon fractions
18 Spinning snack decider
20 Weighing scales
22 Measuring
24 Smoothie sums
26 Shapes
28 Marshmallow shapes
30 Tessellating biscuits

2 Toys and games

36 Joan Clarke
38 Cipher wheel
40 Adding
41 Subtracting
42 Animal number bonds
44 Make your own currency
48 Multiplication
50 Dividing clay
52 Division

3 Out and about

56 Buildings
58 Zaha Hadid
60 Shape city
66 Möbius loop
68 Rainwater measures
70 Natural symmetry
72 Rotating starfish
74 Nature array
76 Times-table flowers

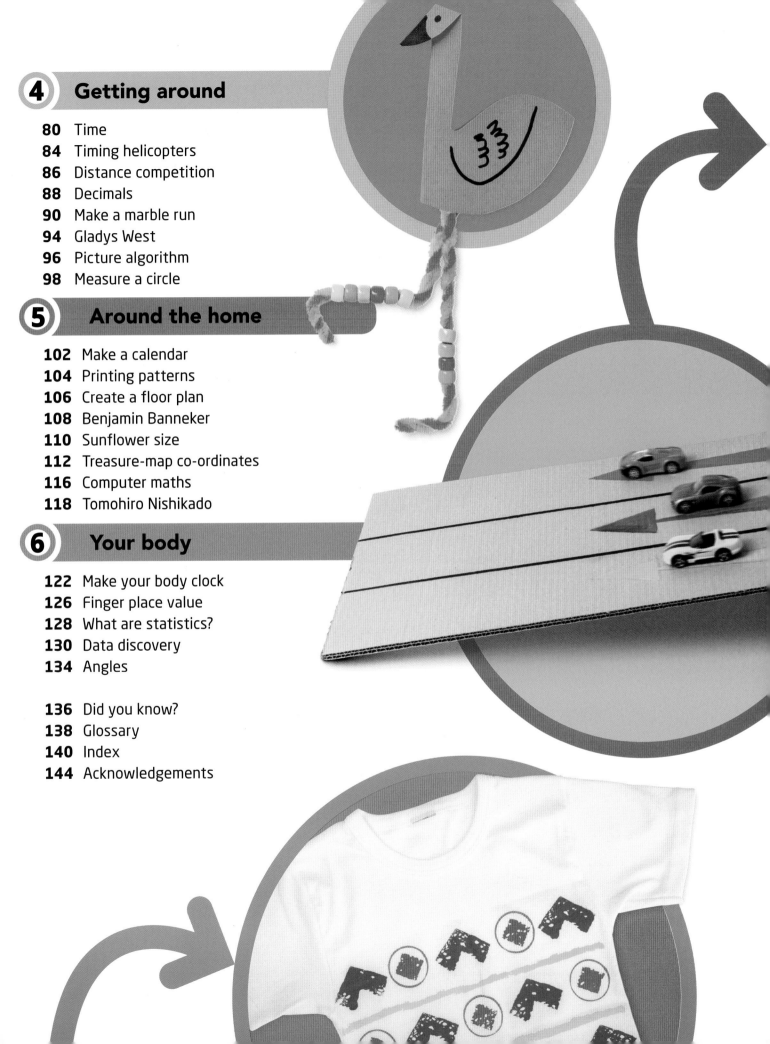

4 Getting around

80 Time
84 Timing helicopters
86 Distance competition
88 Decimals
90 Make a marble run
94 Gladys West
96 Picture algorithm
98 Measure a circle

5 Around the home

102 Make a calendar
104 Printing patterns
106 Create a floor plan
108 Benjamin Banneker
110 Sunflower size
112 Treasure-map co-ordinates
116 Computer maths
118 Tomohiro Nishikado

6 Your body

122 Make your body clock
126 Finger place value
128 What are statistics?
130 Data discovery
134 Angles

136 Did you know?
138 Glossary
140 Index
144 Acknowledgements

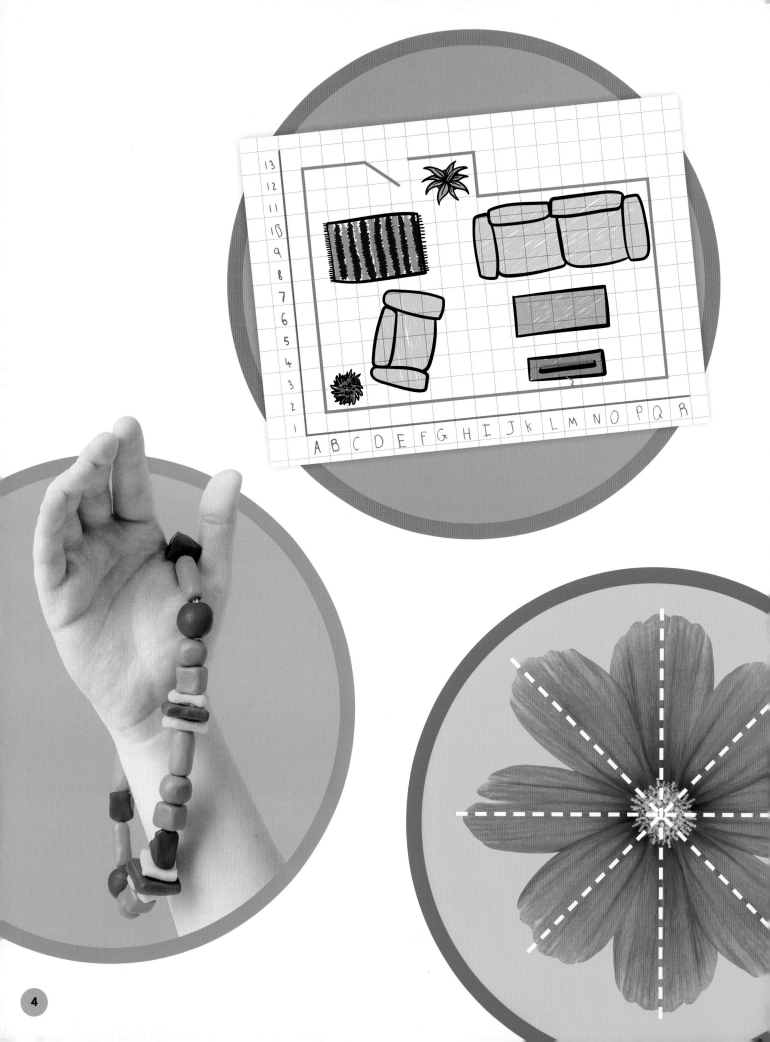

I was excited to write this book and share my love of maths with you. It's something that has fascinated me since I was your age and continues to amaze me with every new thing I learn.

Maths is about solving problems and being creative. The world is full of problems waiting to be solved. Many people around the world work as scientists, engineers, technologists, and in hospitals – all of them use maths skills to help people and create solutions. I hope you'll be able to use your creativity as you try the activities packed into this book.

As you turn the pages you'll realise that maths isn't just about the classroom or homework. It's all over our world and is done by almost everyone every day. The food you eat, the buildings you visit, and your body itself – all are made possible by a fantastic balance of mathematics. Maths shows up everywhere.

Before you get started, I have one special request for you. When you learn a cool new bit of maths, read about an amazing person, or build something new from this book, share it with your friends and family. Help them be maths whizzes with you!

Have conversations with the people around you whenever and wherever you see maths. Keep talking and thinking about it – maybe one day you'll get to write a book about it too.

Anyone can be a maths whizz. Let's get you started!

Anne-Marie Imafidon

Dr. Anne-Marie Imafidon

How this book works

In *How to be a Maths Whizz,* you will learn how to think and act like a mathematician. The book is packed with fun activities, important topics, and people who have used their maths skills to do amazing things.

Awesome activities

Learn on the job with the activities throughout this book, which show key ideas within maths. There are also crafts to make maths devices, such as an abacus, and memory aids that help you remember important facts.

Everything you need for an activity is listed at the start.

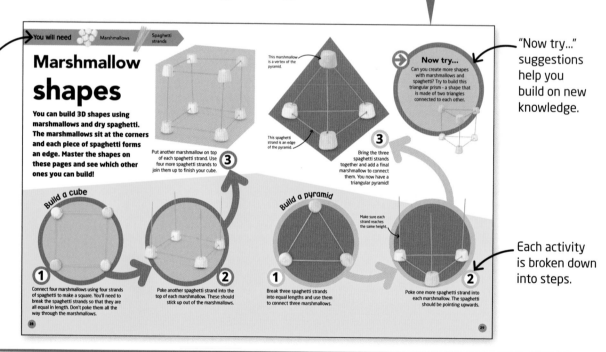

"Now try..." suggestions help you build on new knowledge.

Each activity is broken down into steps.

Safety first

All of the projects in this book should be done with care. If you see this symbol at the top of a page, it means that you will need an adult to help you with the activity.

Take particular care when:

• you are using sharp objects, such as scissors

• you are running around with friends

• you are handling hot food

• you are outside – always tell an adult what you are doing

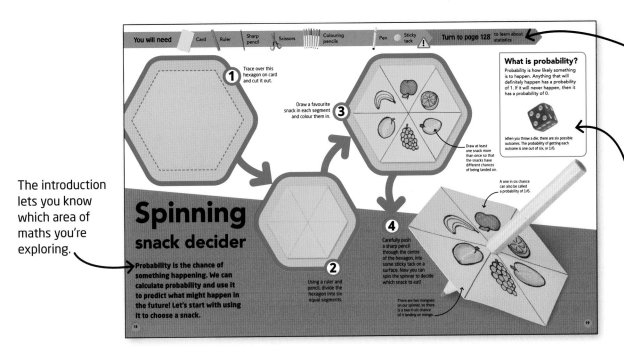

Turn to page 128 to learn about statistics

Look out for "Turn to..." bars, leading you to related pages.

Feature boxes provide more information about the maths behind the activity.

The introduction lets you know which area of maths you're exploring.

Top topics

Learn about some of the key maths topics, such as division, measuring, and decimals. These will support and build on what you've learned through the craft projects.

Maths heroes

Meet the inspirational people who have used maths to make a difference in the world. And remember: anyone can learn to be a maths whizz.

Getting ready

You'll need pens and pencils to write out sums, make notes, and draw shapes.

You can do many of the activities in this book straight away. Rummage around at home to see if you can gather the items you need. Here are instructions on how to use some of the most important maths tools you'll need.

You'll need scissors to cut things out.

A ruler will help you draw straight lines and measure things.

Using a protractor

A protractor can help you draw an angle of a certain size. Follow these steps to learn how.

1 Draw a straight line with a dot on the end. This will be the first line of your angle and its vertex (corner).

2 Line up the protractor's centre point with the dot, and the starting line of your angle with the baseline.

3 Draw a dot above the measurement showing the size of the angle you want to draw.

4 Draw a line between the dots to create your angle!

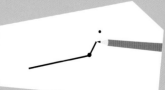

For angles facing the right, use these measurements.

For angles facing the left, use these measurements.

Baseline

Centre point

Tracing

You can transfer a shape from this book onto paper or card by tracing it. You'll need tracing paper, a sharp pencil, a soft graphite pencil (such as 6B) and the steps below.

1 Place the tracing paper over the shape and draw over the lines using any pencil.

2 Flip the tracing paper. Shade over the back of the lines with a soft graphite pencil.

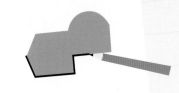

3 Place the tracing paper, shaded side down, onto the paper or card you're tracing onto.

4 Pressing down with a sharp pencil, draw over the lines of the shape to transfer it.

Calculators

Calculators help us to work out sums quickly. To use one, press the buttons that show the numbers and symbols in a sum, in order. Then, press the "=" button to show the answer.

To clear away a sum and start a new one, press this button.

For 45 x 7, you would press "4" and "5" to make 45, then "x", then "7", and finally the "=" symbol.

For numbers with more than one digit, press each digit in the number, from left to right. So, for "52", you'd press "5" and then "2".

Always press "=" at the end of the sum.

Tessellation

Counting

Halving

Probability

Edible maths

If you look closely, there's maths involved with how food looks, the way it's made, and in sharing it out. From making recipes to describing the shape of your favourite snack, learn to see the maths behind the food on your plate.

Doubling

Measuring

Fractions

Shapes

Whole numbers

We count things one by one. If you have a whole satsuma and another whole satsuma – that's two satsumas. We might count up fruit, vegetables, or other items of food if we're following a recipe.

1

2

3

4

5

10

Counting

You've probably been counting since you were little. It's a simple way of finding how many of something you have. Everyday life is full of counting. If you want to give each of your friends an orange, you'd count the oranges up. You'd need to count a lot more pieces of food if you were giving one to everybody in your school!

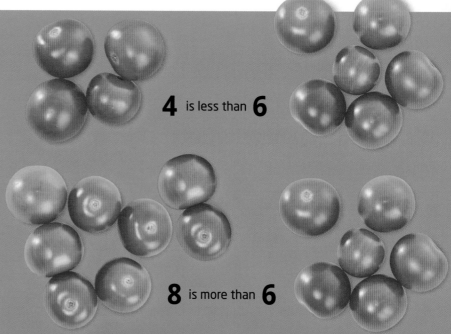

4 is less than 6

8 is more than 6

More than or less than?

Finding out if one number is bigger than another is called comparing numbers. For example, two is more than one. This type of maths is useful in real life if you need to check you've shared something out fairly. If you take six tomatoes and your friend is left with four, then you have taken more tomatoes than your friend.

Place value

All numbers are written using one or more of the same 10 digits – 0, 1, 2, 3, 4, 5, 6, 7, 8 and 9. However, the value of each digit in a number depends on its position in that number. This is called its place value. A "1" at the start of a three-digit number is worth more than if it were at the end!

The "1" in 136 biscuits stands for 100 biscuits.

The "3" in 136 biscuits stands for 30 biscuits.

The "6" in 136 biscuits stands for 6 biscuits.

100s	10s	1s
1	3	6

What's it worth?

If you write down that you have 136 biscuits, the first number, "1", has a place value of 100; the middle number, "3", has a place value of 30 (3 lots of 10); and the last number, "6", is the number of biscuits less than 10 – making a total of 136.

Counting fractions

A fraction is part of a whole. Numbers less than one are fractions. You can count up fractions until you get a whole number. If you count the sections in a pizza, you're counting fractions!

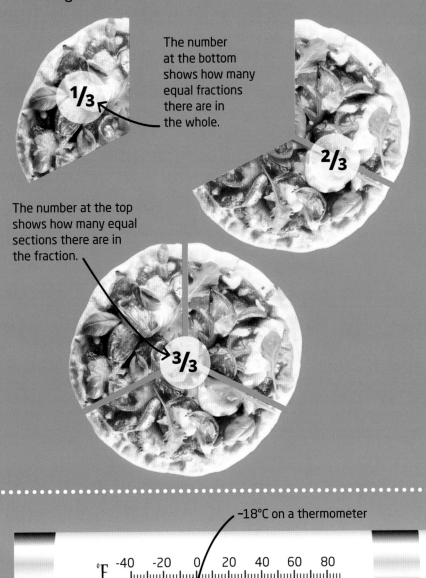

The number at the bottom shows how many equal fractions there are in the whole.

1/3

2/3

The number at the top shows how many equal sections there are in the fraction.

3/3

−18°C on a thermometer

°F -40 -20 0 20 40 60 80

°C -40 -30 -20 -10 0 10 20

Negative numbers

You can count down as well as up. When you count below zero, you are counting in negative numbers. These have a minus sign (-) in front of them. You may see negative numbers used for temperatures. It's probably –18°C in your freezer. This is the perfect temperature for keeping frozen food.

Edible abacus

Make sure the holes in both tubes line up with one another.

1 Use the pointy end of a skewer to poke five holes down the side of each kitchen-roll tube.

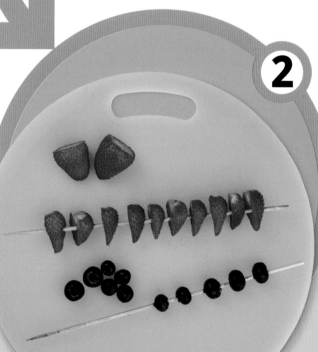

2 Thread 10 pieces of the same fruit onto a skewer. Then, make four more skewers, each with a different fruit.

3 Put a fruit skewer into each hole of one tube. Push the other side of the skewers into the holes in the other tube to finish your edible abacus.

Using fingers and toes to count very small numbers is all very well, but what about bigger numbers? An abacus is an object that helps you with more difficult counting, as well as adding and subtracting.

How do you use it?

The rows are worth different amounts, as shown on the picture below. To show a number, begin with all the fruit on the left. Then, move across each digit in the number, using the matching row. For 11,111, you would move one of each row across!

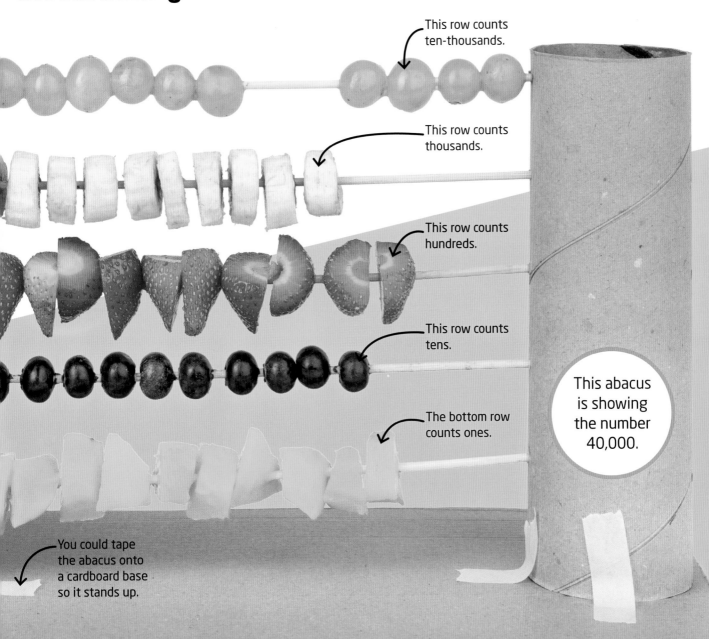

This row counts ten-thousands.

This row counts thousands.

This row counts hundreds.

This row counts tens.

The bottom row counts ones.

This abacus is showing the number 40,000.

You could tape the abacus onto a cardboard base so it stands up.

You will need

Four paper plates

Paint

Paint brush

Ruler

Pencil

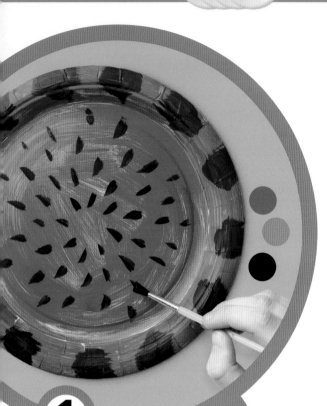

1

Paint a paper plate so it looks like the inside of a watermelon.

Watermelon fractions

What do a slice of pizza and an orange segment have in common? They're both fractions! When we split something up into parts, we create fractions. Here's how you can split up a watermelon plate.

Carefully cut along the line to divide it into two halves.

3

Turn the plate over. Use a pencil and a ruler to draw a thin line down the middle.

2

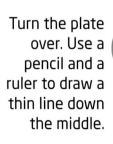

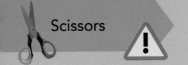

Two halves

Four quarters

Eight eighths

4 Make two more watermelon plates, but cut them into quarters and eighths. Write the fraction on the back of each piece. One half is written as ½, one quarter is written as ¼, and one eighth is written as ⅛. See what fractions you can combine to make a whole plate.

This is a quarter of the watermelon plate. Four quarters make up one plate. Two quarters make up one half.

Some of these fractions have the same value as each other, or are equivalent, such as two eighths and one quarter.

Now try...

You can halve the eighths again to make sixteenths. One sixteenth is written as ¹⁄₁₆.

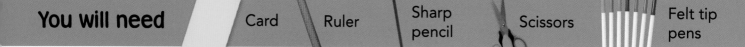
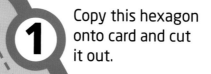

1 Copy this hexagon onto card and cut it out.

3 Draw a favourite snack in each segment and colour them in.

2 Using a ruler and pencil, divide the hexagon into six equal segments.

Spinning
snack decider

Probability is the chance of something happening. We can calculate probability and use it to predict what might happen in the future! Let's start with using it to choose a snack.

18

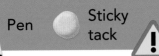

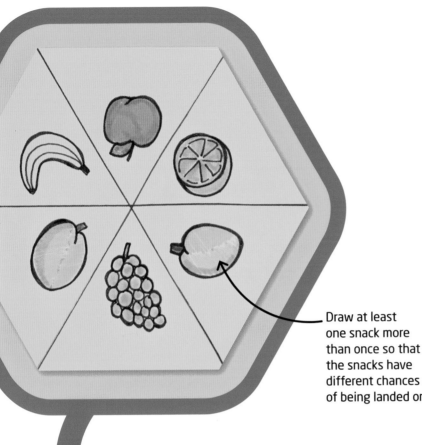

Draw at least one snack more than once so that the snacks have different chances of being landed on.

What is probability?

Probability is how likely something is to happen. Anything that will definitely happen has a probability of one. If it will never happen, then it has a probability of zero.

When you throw a die, there are six possible outcomes. The probability of getting each outcome is one out of six, or 1/6.

A one in six chance can also be called a probability of 1/6.

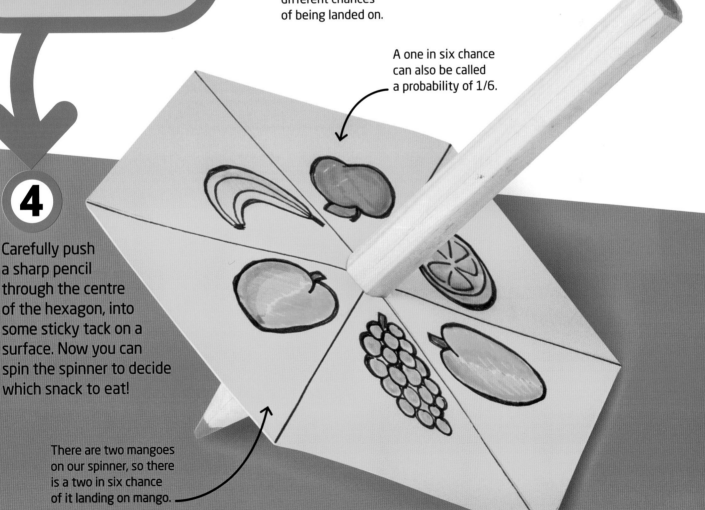

4

Carefully push a sharp pencil through the centre of the hexagon, into some sticky tack on a surface. Now you can spin the spinner to decide which snack to eat!

There are two mangoes on our spinner, so there is a two in six chance of it landing on mango.

You will need

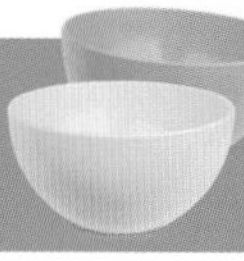

Two plastic bowls of the same weight

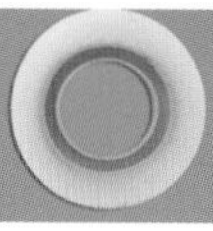

Tape

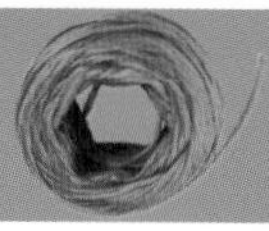

String

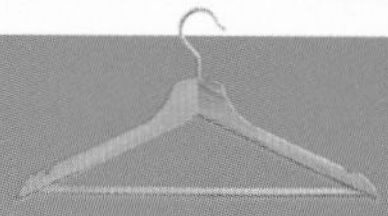

Coat hanger

Weighing scales

Weight (heaviness) is measured using a device called scales. Follow the steps on these pages to make your very own scales, and find out which is heavier out of your things. If you know the weight of something, you can find something else that weighs the same.

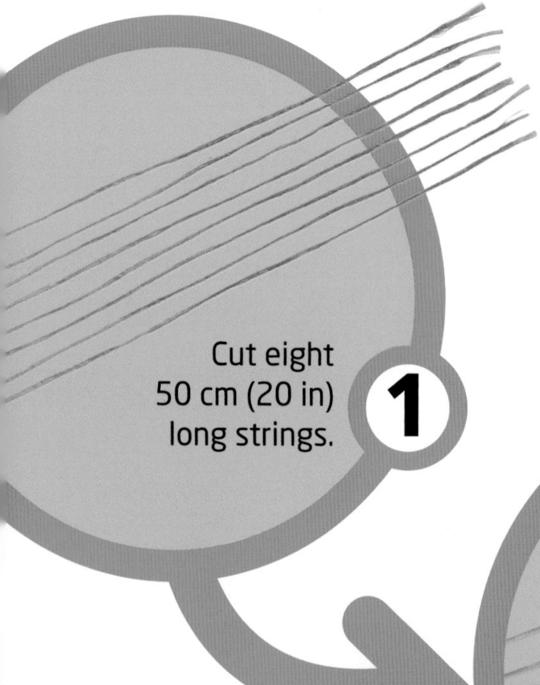

1 Cut eight 50 cm (20 in) long strings.

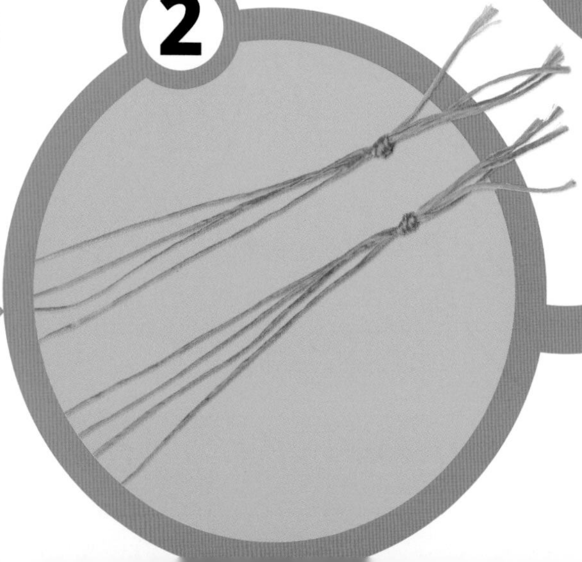

2 Tie four strings together at one end. Repeat for the last four strings.

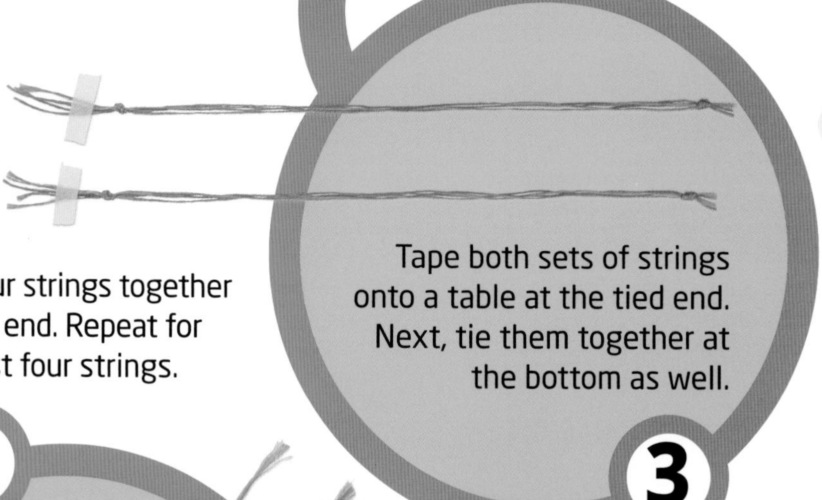

3 Tape both sets of strings onto a table at the tied end. Next, tie them together at the bottom as well.

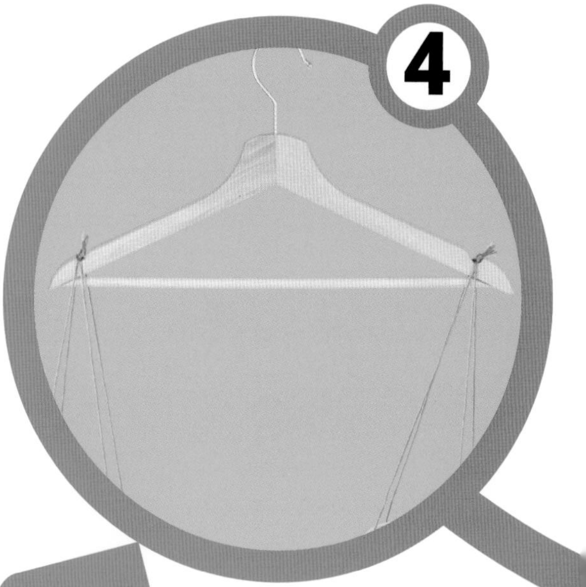

4 Remove the strings from the table and hang them off either end of the coathanger, in the grooves if it has them. Tape them down.

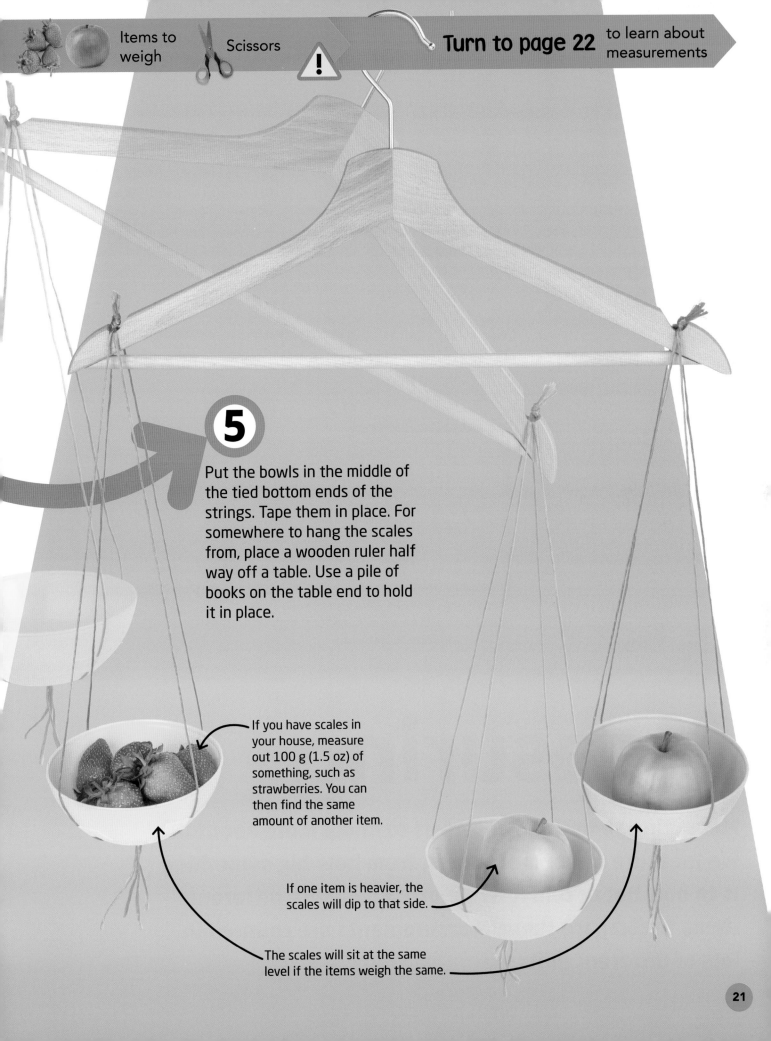

5

Put the bowls in the middle of the tied bottom ends of the strings. Tape them in place. For somewhere to hang the scales from, place a wooden ruler half way off a table. Use a pile of books on the table end to hold it in place.

If you have scales in your house, measure out 100 g (1.5 oz) of something, such as strawberries. You can then find the same amount of another item.

If one item is heavier, the scales will dip to that side.

The scales will sit at the same level if the items weigh the same.

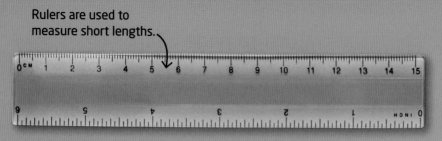

Rulers are used to measure short lengths.

Length

How tall are you? This is an example of length. In countries that use metric measurements, length is measured in centimetres (cm), metres (m), and kilometres (km). In countries that use imperial units, length can be measured in inches (in), feet (ft), and miles (mi).

Volume

How much liquid have you drunk today? Liquid is measured in volume. In countries that use metric measurements, volume is measured in millilitres (ml) or litres (l). In countries that use imperial units, volume can be measured in fluid ounces (fluid oz) or pints (pt).

Area

How big is this page? The total size of a flat shape is called its area. In countries that use metric units, area is measured in square centimetres (cm^2) or square metres (m^2). In countries that use imperial units, area is measured in square inches (in^2) or square feet (ft^2).

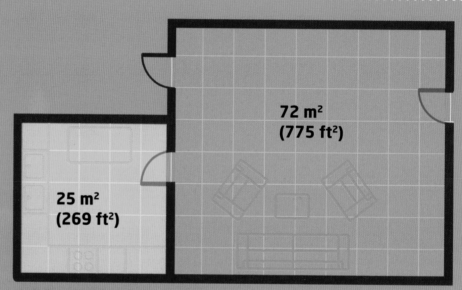

72 m^2 (775 ft^2)

25 m^2 (269 ft^2)

Building designs include area to show that rooms will be big enough for things such as furniture to fit inside.

Measuring

Measuring something allows us to know more about it. We measure all sorts of things, from how big something is to how hot or cold it is. We often measure different items to compare them. Measurements are counted in lots of different units.

The volume of juice needs to be known to add water.

The right volume of water is needed.

We might measure volume when diluting drinks.

Weight

How heavy are you? This is your weight. In countries that use metric measurements, weight is usually measured in milligrams (mg), grams (g), and kilograms (kg). In countries that use imperial measurements, weight is usually measured in pounds (lb) and ounces (oz).

Temperature

How hot or cold is it in your room? This is the temperature. In countries that use metric measurements, temperature is measured in degrees Celsius (°C). In countries that use imperial measurements, temperature is measured in Fahrenheit (°F).

Fahrenheit, or °F

Celsius, or °C

This dial points to the weight of your objects.

The outer ring has measurements in grams and kilograms.

The inner ring has measurements in ounces and pounds.

Time

How long has it been since you woke up? This is an example of time. We measure the passing of time in seconds, minutes, hours, days, weeks, and years.

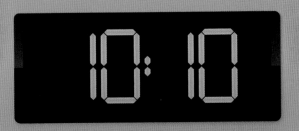

23

Smoothie sums

Halving and doubling

Halving means splitting – or dividing – something equally in two. Doubling means adding the same amount of something again, which is a type of maths called multiplication.

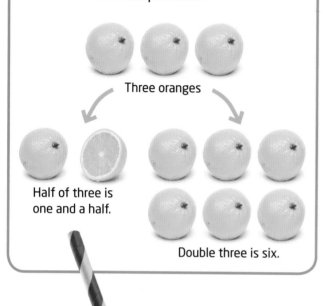

Three oranges

Half of three is one and a half.

Double three is six.

Follow the recipe to make a glass of delicious fruit smoothie. Then, learn how to change the recipe to make half as much, for when you're not feeling very thirsty. Finally, find out how to make double the amount, so you can give a glass to a lucky friend!

1

120 ml of yoghurt

120 ml of milk

Four strawberries, sliced

One banana, peeled and sliced

Blend these ingredients to make one large glass of smoothie.

2

If you want to make half a glass of smoothie, you need to halve the amounts in step one.

To make two smoothies, double the amounts in step one.

Now try...

Can you work out how many strawberries you would need to make four smoothies?

Shapes

Some shapes are flat objects that you can draw. Others aren't flat, such as the shape of an orange. You can spot different shapes by their features. They might have straight lines, curved lines, lots of lines, or very few lines!

Shapes in real life

Everything has a shape – just think about a plate of food! Cookies tend to be circles and slices of round fruit can look like ovals. From above, some berries look like circles, flapjacks often look like rectangles, and cheese slices might look like triangles. Try spotting shapes around you to help learn the number of sides, corners, and edges linked with each one.

2D or 3D?

These are two types of shape. Flat shapes are called two dimensional (2D). They only exist in two directions – left to right and top to bottom. Shapes with three directions are called three dimensional (3D). These have the directions left to right, top to bottom, and front to back.

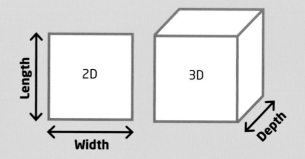

Some 2D shapes

We can tell a shape by how many edges (lines) it has, and how many corners (where two lines meet) it has.

A pentagon has five sides.

Pentagon

A hexagon has six sides.

Hexagon

An octagon has eight sides.

Octagon

All triangles have three sides.

All squares and rectangles have four sides.

Rectangles and squares have four corners.

A circle has one curved edge all the way round.

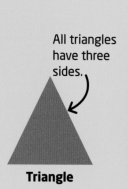

Triangle

Square

Rectangle

Circle

Closed 2D shapes with multiple straight edges are called **polygons**.

Maryam Mirzakhani

The mathematical study of shapes is called geometry. Maryam Mirzakhani was a famous geometrist who spent lots of time studying one-dimensional surfaces. These are surfaces made up of a single line. She won an important maths award for her work, called the Fields Medal.

- Maryam Mirzakhani
- 1977–2017
- From Iran

Cuboids and cubes have six faces.

Cube

Cylinders have two edges.

Cylinder

Some 3D shapes

3D shapes have height, width, and length. Each corner is called a vertex, each side is called a face, and in between faces there are edges. Spheroids only have one face and no edges or vertices.

Cuboid

Spheroid

Cone

Marshmallow shapes

You can build 3D shapes using marshmallows and dry spaghetti. The marshmallows sit at the corners and each piece of spaghetti forms an edge. Master the shapes on these pages and see which other ones you can build!

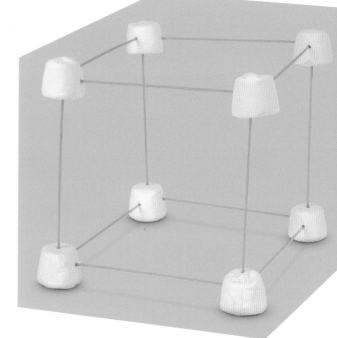

Put another marshmallow on top of each spaghetti strand. Use four more spaghetti strands to join them up to finish your cube.

3

Build a cube

1

Connect four marshmallows using four strands of spaghetti to make a square. You'll need to break the spaghetti strands so that they are all equal in length. Don't poke them all the way through the marshmallows.

2

Poke another spaghetti strand into the top of each marshmallow. These should stick up out of the marshmallows.

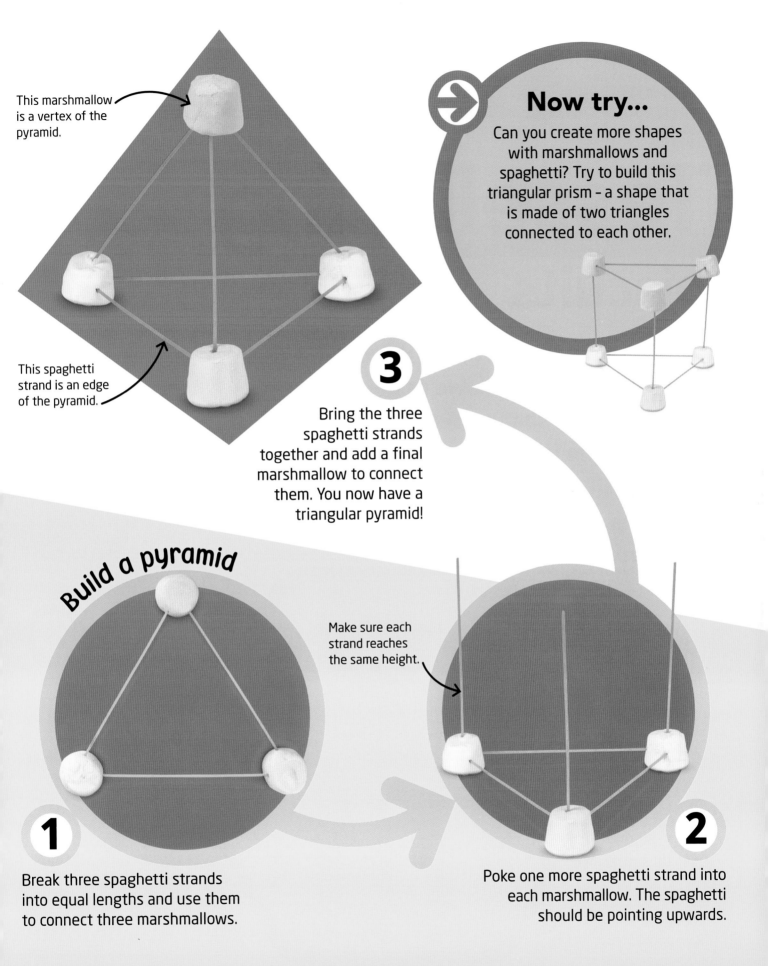

This marshmallow is a vertex of the pyramid.

This spaghetti strand is an edge of the pyramid.

→ **Now try...**
Can you create more shapes with marshmallows and spaghetti? Try to build this triangular prism - a shape that is made of two triangles connected to each other.

3
Bring the three spaghetti strands together and add a final marshmallow to connect them. You now have a triangular pyramid!

Build a pyramid

Make sure each strand reaches the same height.

1
Break three spaghetti strands into equal lengths and use them to connect three marshmallows.

2
Poke one more spaghetti strand into each marshmallow. The spaghetti should be pointing upwards.

You will need
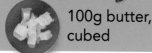

Large mixing bowl

Electric mixer or hand whisk

Wooden spoon

Sieve

Ingredients

100g butter, cubed

1 large egg

135g caster sugar

½ teaspoon vanilla extract

Tessellating
biscuits

When shapes fit together without gaps, it's called tessellation. We're going to make some hexagon-shaped biscuits. Can you arrange them in a tessellating pattern?

2

Stir in the sugar and vanilla extract. Sift in the flour a little at a time. Work it in until a soft dough forms.

1

Preheat the oven to 180°C (350°F). Beat the butter and egg together using a wooden spoon, until it's light and fluffy.

Cookie cutter

2 baking trays

Grease-proof paper

Wire cooling rack

Oven

150g self-raising flour

Icing sugar and food colouring

Sugar

Vanilla extract

3 Cover the dough and put it in the fridge. After 30 minutes, take it out and transfer it to a clean surface. Roll the dough out until it's flat, using flour to stop it sticking to things.

4 Use the cutter to cut out the biscuits.

Space out the biscuits on baking trays lined with baking paper. Bake in the oven for 15 minutes, then transfer to a wire rack to cool.

5

6

Follow the instructions on the icing-sugar packet to make icing. Divide the icing into two bowls and add a few drops of different food colouring to each.

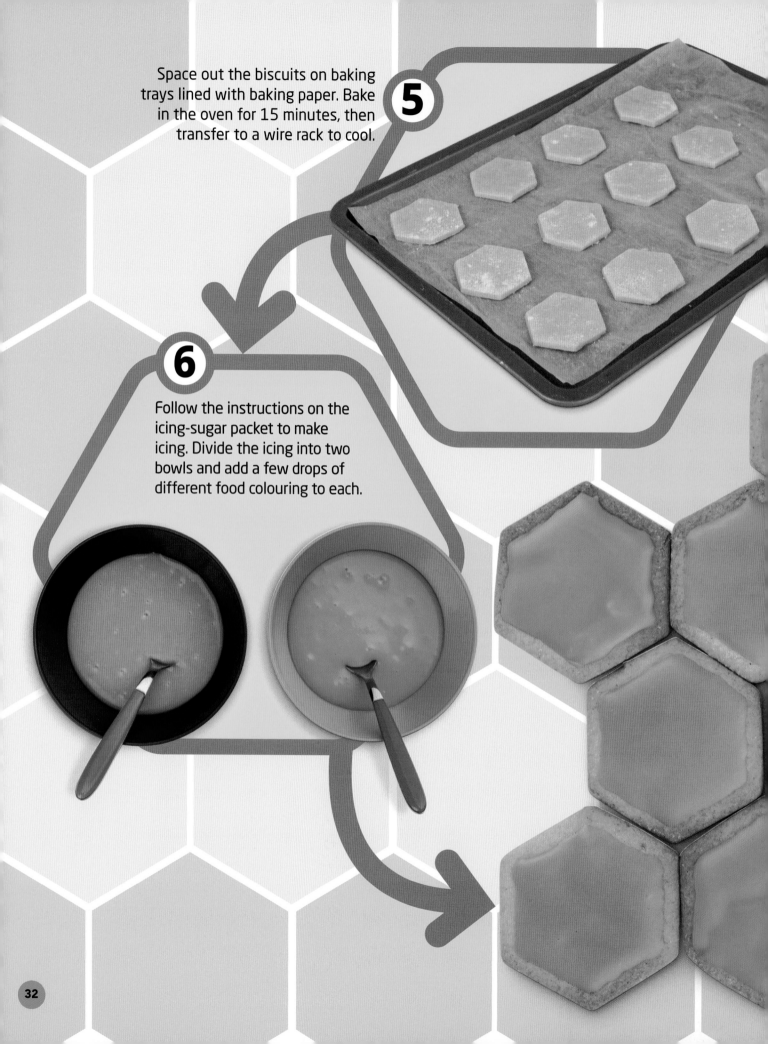

Tessellation in design

Maths can inspire clothing designs. The houndstooth pattern uses tessellating shapes and has been around for over 2,000 years. The same distinct shape appears in alternating colours, without gaps, across the design.

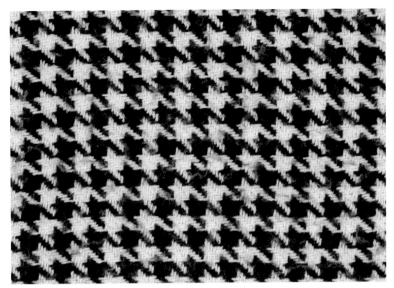

The houndstooth pattern

7 Ice an equal amount of biscuits in each colour and arrange them in a tessellating pattern, like this!

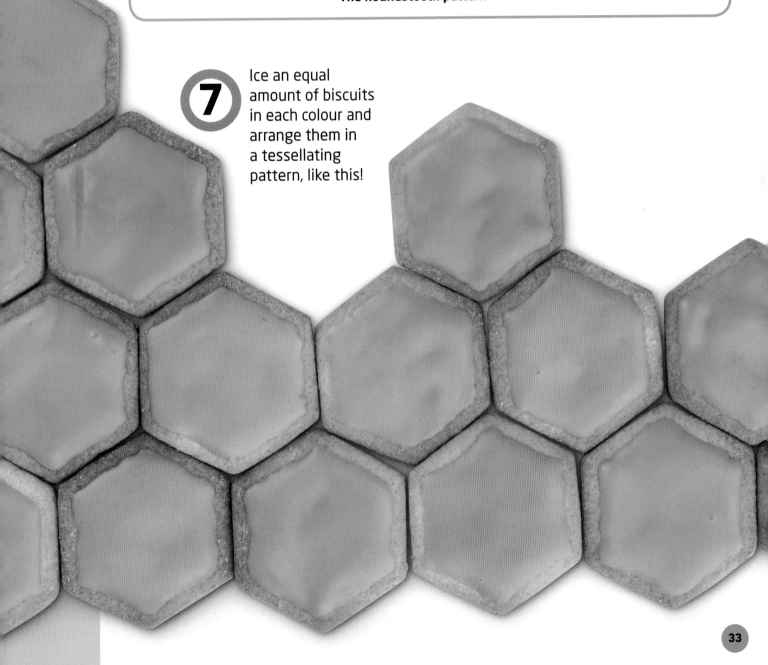

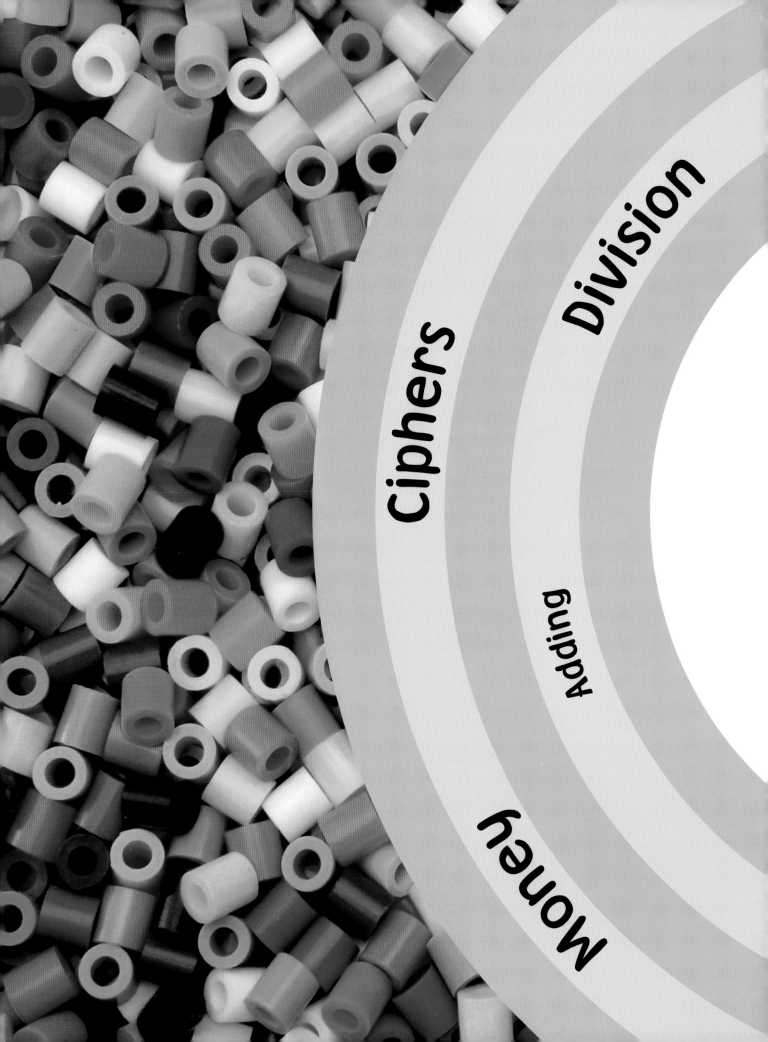

Division

Ciphers

Adding

Money

Toys and games

You might use maths without thinking about it, even while you're playing! You could use the skill of counting to make a secret code, or division to break up a lump of clay. We can even use maths to make up new games and activities.

Joan Clarke

Codebreaker • 1917–1996 • From the UK

....

Joan studied maths at university and went on to work for the British government during the Second World War (WWII). She used her mathematical mind to help work out the codes in which enemy messages were written. The work done by the codebreakers helped to end the war more quickly.

Codebreakers

Joan worked at Bletchley Park in the UK, where British codebreakers tried to understand enemy messages. She was specially recruited to work there by one of her university teachers in 1940, who was impressed by Joan's mathematical skills. Together with other codebreakers, Joan worked day and night to crack the cryptic codes.

Joan used maths involving probability (the likelihood of something happening) to help work out codes.

Cipher maths

A cipher is a system of changing letters in a message to make it secret. Maths is often used to create these codes. For example, you could replace a letter with one that appears five letters earlier in the alphabet. Joan worked on very complicated ciphers during WWII.

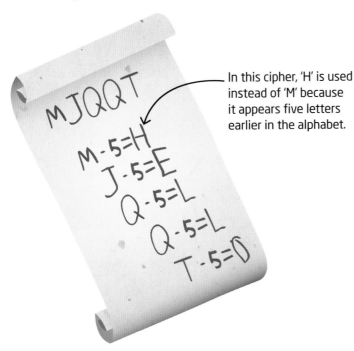

In this cipher, 'H' is used instead of 'M' because it appears five letters earlier in the alphabet.

MJQQT

M - 5 = H
J - 5 = E
Q - 5 = L
Q - 5 = L
T - 5 = O

Enigma code

Enemy codes were made using a clever machine, called Enigma. They simply typed in a message, and the machine turned it into an extremely complex code. Eventually, a special computer was built at Bletchley Park which cracked the Enigma code.

Dangerous secrets

Cracking codes helped the British Navy find out the location of dangerous enemy submarines – and avoid them.

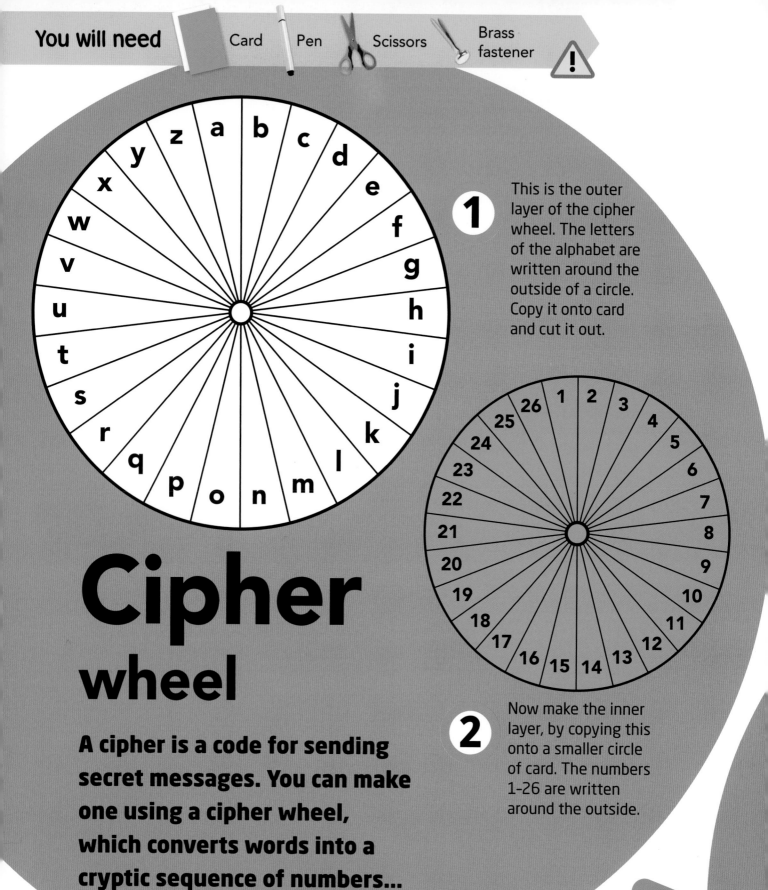

① This is the outer layer of the cipher wheel. The letters of the alphabet are written around the outside of a circle. Copy it onto card and cut it out.

② Now make the inner layer, by copying this onto a smaller circle of card. The numbers 1–26 are written around the outside.

Cipher wheel

A cipher is a code for sending secret messages. You can make one using a cipher wheel, which converts words into a cryptic sequence of numbers...

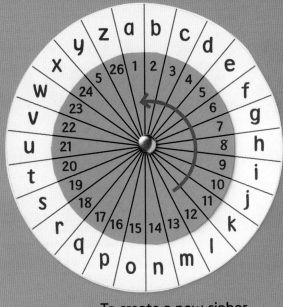

How to use it

1) Move the inside wheel to a new position.

2) Find the numbers to go with each letter in your message, and write them down.

3) Pass the cipher wheel to a friend, along with the message.

4) Challenge your friend to decode (work out) what you've written!

12 4 4 19 26 19 19 7 4
15 11 26 24 7 14 20 18 4
(meet at the playhouse)

This cipher uses the number 26 as the letter "a".

4 To create a new cipher, move the wheels so that the numbers match up with different letters. You can make 26 codes!

Place the smaller circle in the centre of the larger one. Push the fastener through both circles, into a piece of sticky tack on a surface. Bend back the legs of the fastener to secure it.

3

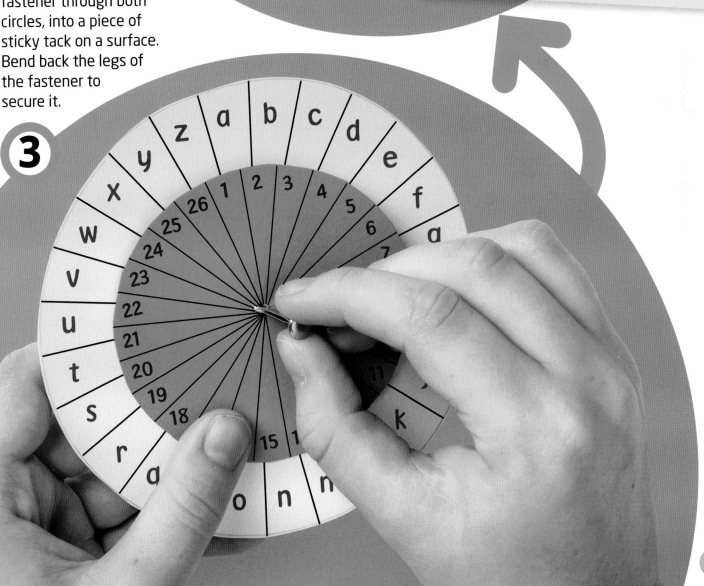

You have two balls.

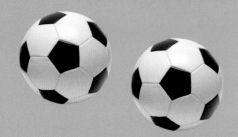

Adding

Adding is when you put numbers or things together to make a larger number or larger group of things.

You get three more balls. How many balls are there altogether?

You can show this as an **addition** calculation.

$$2 + 3 = 5$$

This symbol means **added to** or **plus**.

This symbol means **equals**.

Number lines

Arranging numbers in order along a line helps you to add and subtract. Use a finger to find the first number in your calculation. To add a number, use your finger to count that amount to the right. To subtract a number, count that amount to the left.

To add three to two, move three to the right from two.

| 0 | 1 | 2 | 3 | 4 | 5 |

$$2 + 3 = 5$$

You have six balls.

Subtracting

Subtracting is when you take away a number or part of a group of things to leave a smaller number or group.

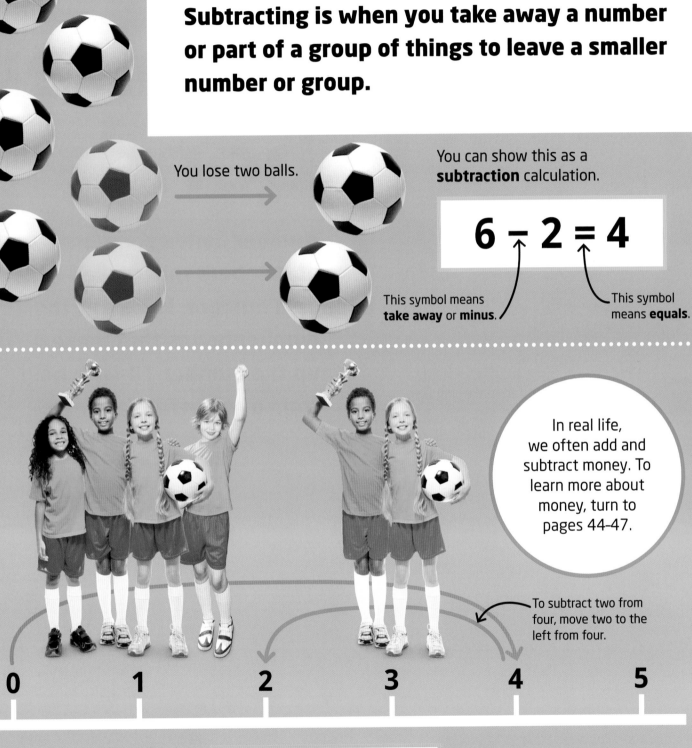

You lose two balls.

You can show this as a **subtraction** calculation.

$$6 - 2 = 4$$

This symbol means **take away** or **minus**.

This symbol means **equals**.

In real life, we often add and subtract money. To learn more about money, turn to pages 44–47.

To subtract two from four, move two to the left from four.

0   1   2   3   4   5

$$4 - 2 = 2$$

Animal number bonds

Number bonds are pairs of numbers that make up a number. Work out the number bonds that make up the number 10 with help from a colourful flamingo.

1 To make the flamingo's body, fold a piece of card in half. Draw the outline of half a flamingo (as below) at the folded edge. Cut along the outline, through both halves of the card.

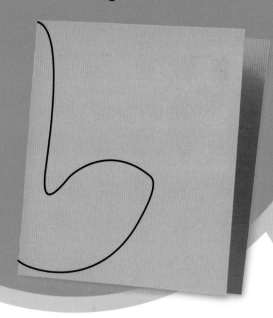

Fold over the top to make the flamingo's head. Use a marker pen to give your flamingo a beak, eyes, and feathers.

2

Get creative with feather patterns on your bird's wings.

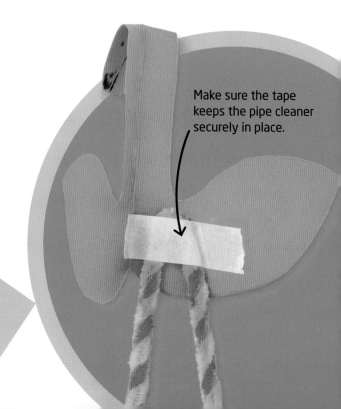

Make sure the tape keeps the pipe cleaner securely in place.

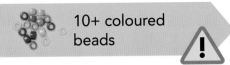
What are number bonds?

The pairs of numbers you can add together to make a specific number are called number bonds. The number four has three number bond pairs. Can you find the number bonds for 15?

$$1 + 3 = 4$$
$$2 + 2 = 4$$
$$4 + 0 = 4$$

→ Now try...

You could make other animals to find the number bonds for different amounts. Try making one that fits 30 beads to learn the number bonds of 30!

Four beads and six beads make 10 beads. This means that four and six are number bonds of 10.

3 Bend a pipe cleaner in half and tape it to the inside of the flamingo to make its legs. Fold the ends of the pipe cleaner into feet.

4 Using 10 beads in total, try out different amounts of beads on each leg until you find all the number bonds of 10! How many pairs can you find?

43

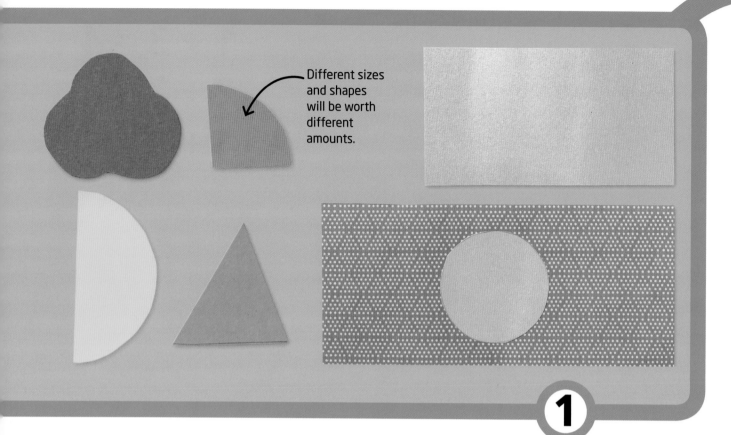

Different sizes and shapes will be worth different amounts.

1

Currency usually comes in coins and notes. Create different shapes of coins from thick coloured paper. Make different sizes of rectangles for the notes.

Make your own currency

Around the world, people use different currencies, or money, to buy and sell things. What currency do you use? Each one has its own name, symbol, and value. Now it's your turn to make a currency – and set up a pretend shop to use it!

Scissors

Turn to page 46 to learn how to use money maths!

2

Coins and notes have symbols on them to show which country they are from. Make up a name and symbol for your currency.

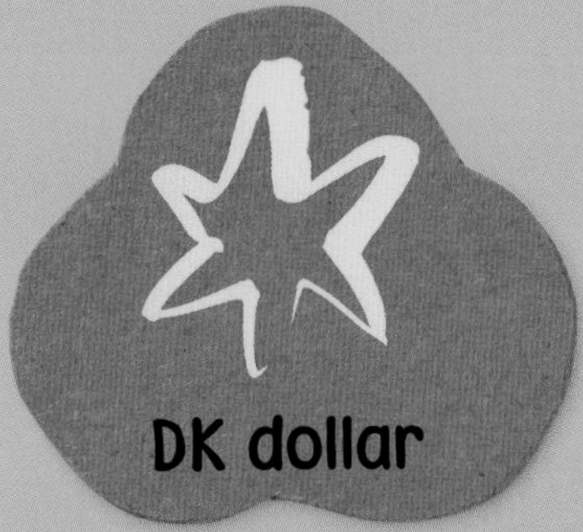
DK dollar

3

Decide what amount each coin or note will be worth, and draw the number and symbol on it. Decorate the money with pictures and colour.

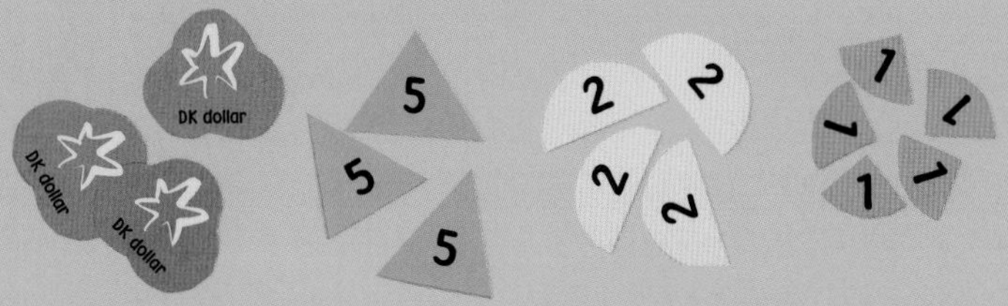
DK dollar
DK dollar
DK dollar
5
5
5
2
2
2
2
1
1
1
1

Some money has important people on it, such as leaders, famous writers, or inventors. You could even put a picture of yourself on it!

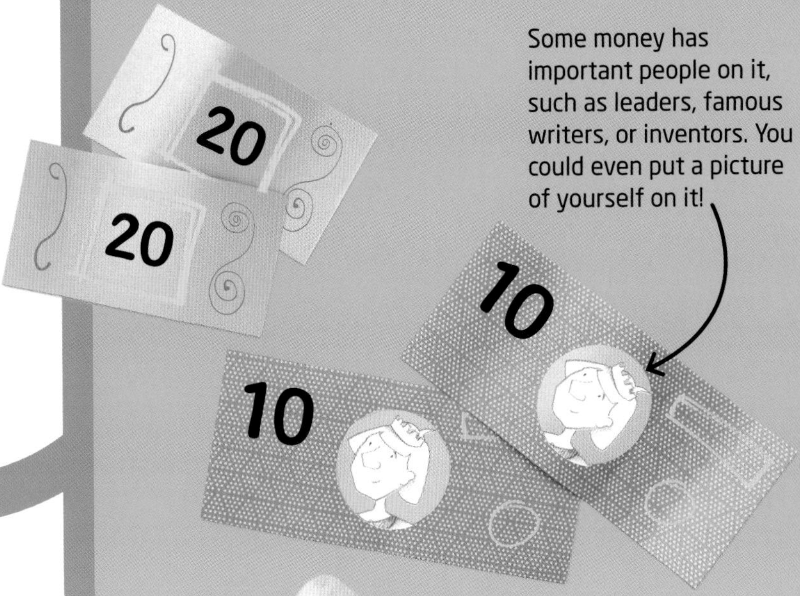
20
20
10
10

4

Set up a pretend shop and "sell" things to your friends (just remember to say you want them back after!).

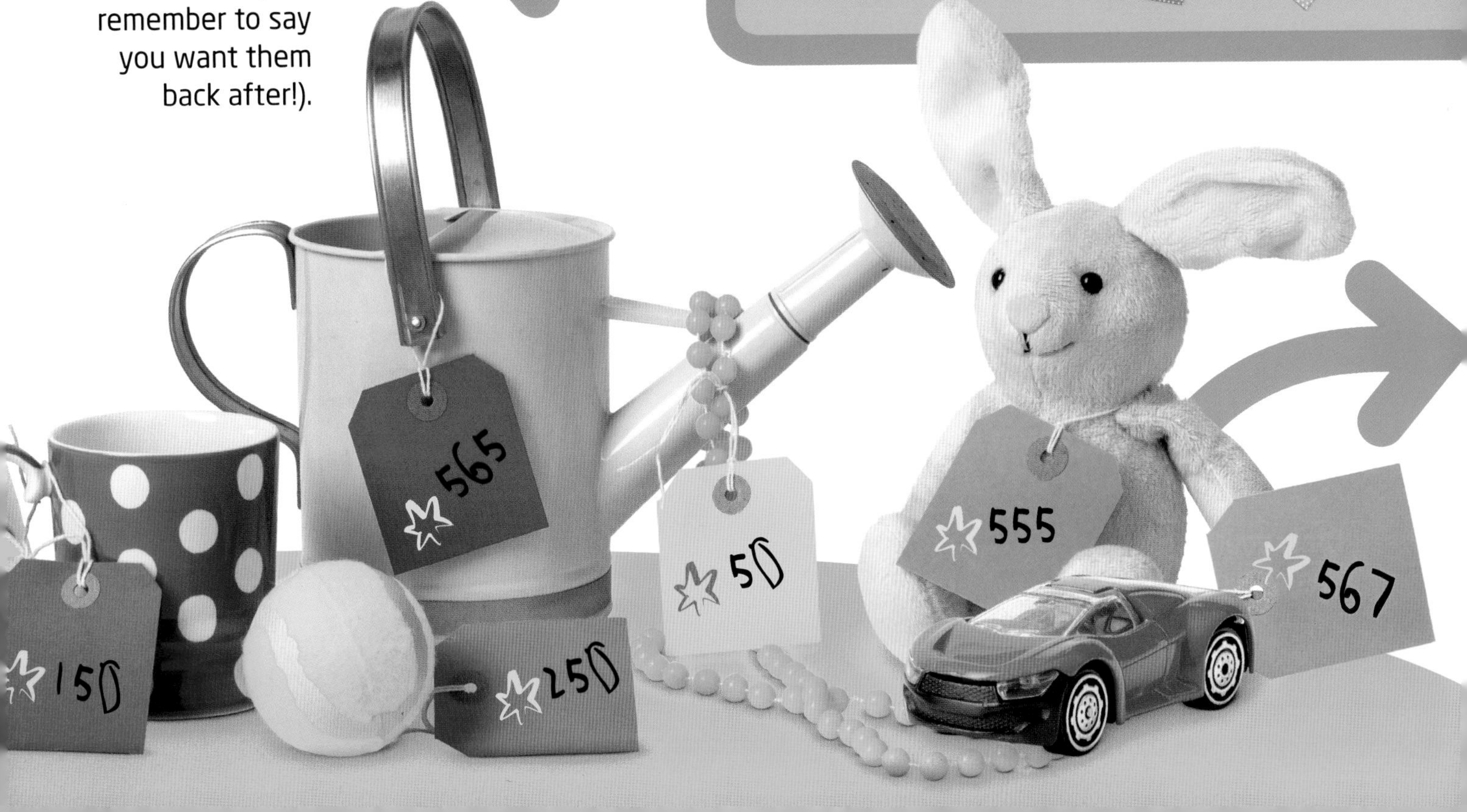
565
50
555
567
150
250

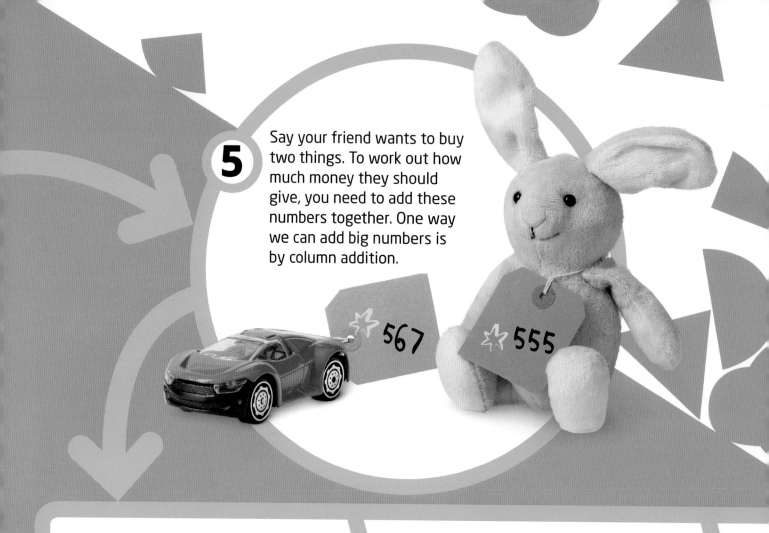

5 Say your friend wants to buy two things. To work out how much money they should give, you need to add these numbers together. One way we can add big numbers is by column addition.

567   555

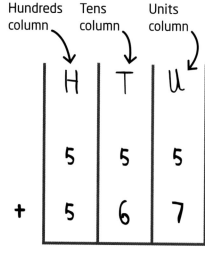

Hundreds column | Tens column | Units column

H T U

   5 5 5

+ 5 6 7

6 Draw your sum on a grid like the one above. Place the digits in separate columns, with the place value of each digit at the top.

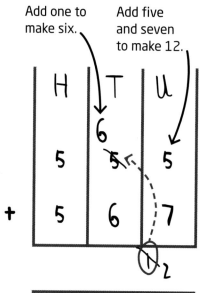

Add one to make six. | Add five and seven to make 12.

H T U

    6

   5 5 5

+ 5 6 7

1 2

7 Add the units together. If the answer has two digits, take the first digit and add it to the top digit in the tens column.

You can use different mathematical strategies to solve sums. For simpler sums, the number lines on pages 40–41 are a great help!

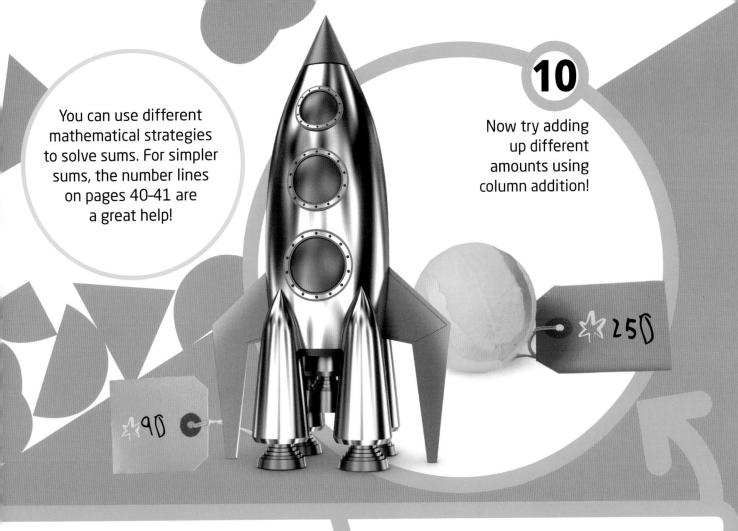

10

Now try adding up different amounts using column addition!

☆ 250

☆ 90

Add six and six to make 12.

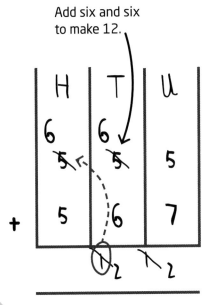

H	T	u
6	6	
5	5	5
+	5	6	7
	1₂ ↗₂	

8

Add the tens together. If the answer has two digits, take the first digit and add it to the top digit in the hundreds column.

Add six and five to make 11.

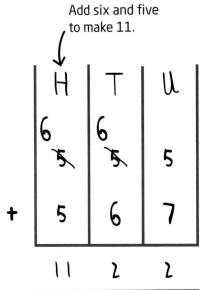

H	T	u
6	6	
5	5	5
+	5	6	7
11	2	2

9

Add the hundreds together. You've now added the sum!

47

Multiplication

You can use multiplication to repeat a group and make a new number. It's the same as adding together lots of the same number. So, 2 multiplied by 3 is the same as 2 + 2 + 2. The symbol that means "multiplied by" is "x".

How many balls?

To find out how many balls there are in this case, you can count them up, or use multiplication. You have four columns of two, which means the answer is 2+2+2+2. This is the same as two multiplied by four, or 2 × 4.

$$2 × 4 = 8$$
$$2 + 2 + 2 + 2 = 8$$

$$6567871 × 0 = 0$$

Multiplying by 0

Multiplying by zero is easy! Zero means nothing. If two multiplied by nothing is the same as zero sets of two, then the answer is nothing. In fact, any number multiplied by zero is zero. Try it on a calculator, with the biggest number you can type.

$$12343 × 1 = 12343$$

Multiplying by 1

Anything multiplied by one is the same number again. This means that the product (the outcome of multiplying) of one and any number is that number. What's the biggest number you can think of? Multiply it by one – it's the same again!

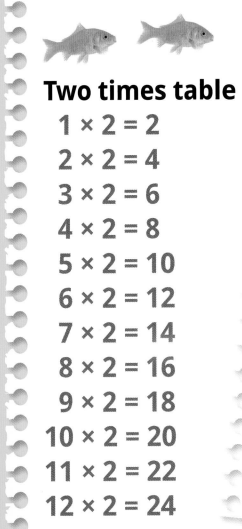

Two times table

$1 \times 2 = 2$

$2 \times 2 = 4$

$3 \times 2 = 6$

$4 \times 2 = 8$

$5 \times 2 = 10$

$6 \times 2 = 12$

$7 \times 2 = 14$

$8 \times 2 = 16$

$9 \times 2 = 18$

$10 \times 2 = 20$

$11 \times 2 = 22$

$12 \times 2 = 24$

Six times table

$1 \times 6 = 6$

$2 \times 6 = 12$

$3 \times 6 = 18$

$4 \times 6 = 24$

$5 \times 6 = 30$

$6 \times 6 = 36$

$7 \times 6 = 42$

$8 \times 6 = 48$

$9 \times 6 = 54$

$10 \times 6 = 60$

$11 \times 6 = 66$

$12 \times 6 = 72$

For the first nine numbers in the 11 times table, repeat the number you're multiplying 11 by. So, 1×11 is 11, 2×11 is 22, and so on!

Times tables

Another way of saying "multiplied by" is to say "times". So, "4×5" can be said as "four times five". A times table contains around the first 12 answers you get from multiplying a number, starting from that number times one. Find the times tables for the numbers one to 12 at the front and back of this book.

Area

The size of a space is called its area. Multiplication can be used to work out area by multiplying the length and the width of a space together. Area is given in squared measurements, which are shown with a '2' next to them.

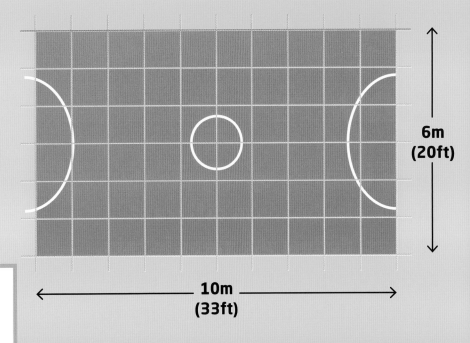

6m
(20ft)

10m
(33ft)

$$6 \text{ m} \times 10 \text{ m} = 60 \text{ m}^2$$

(20 ft × 33 ft = 660 ft²)

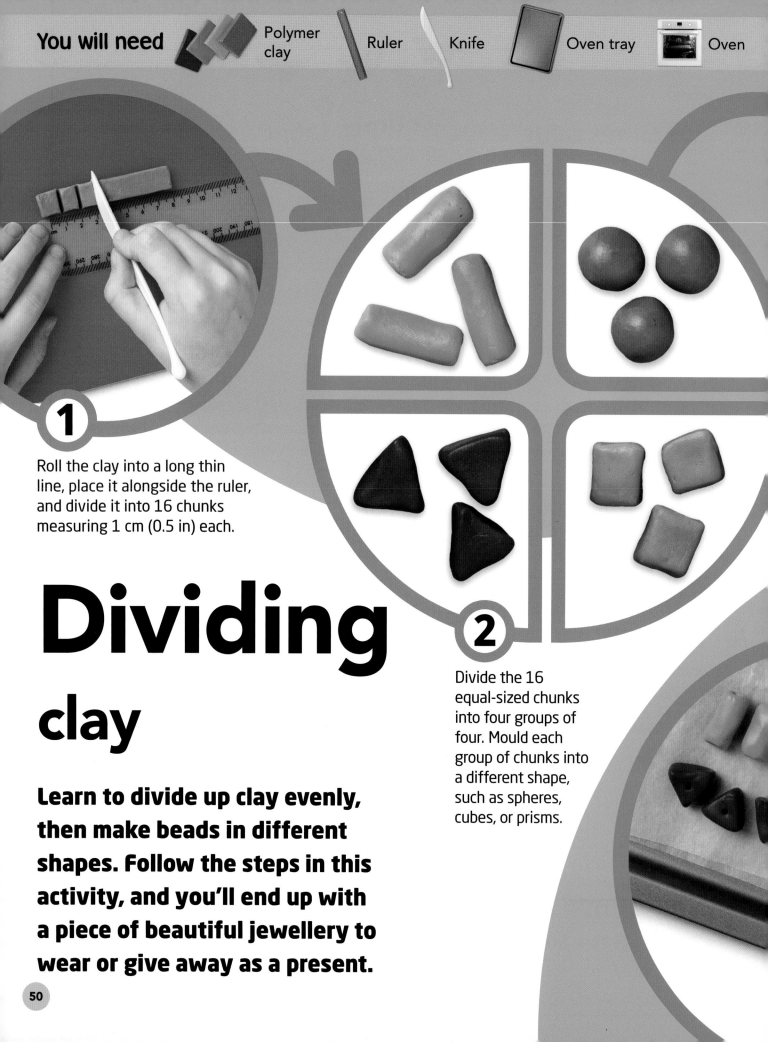

1

Roll the clay into a long thin line, place it alongside the ruler, and divide it into 16 chunks measuring 1 cm (0.5 in) each.

2

Divide the 16 equal-sized chunks into four groups of four. Mould each group of chunks into a different shape, such as spheres, cubes, or prisms.

Dividing clay

Learn to divide up clay evenly, then make beads in different shapes. Follow the steps in this activity, and you'll end up with a piece of beautiful jewellery to wear or give away as a present.

Turn to page 52 to learn more about division.

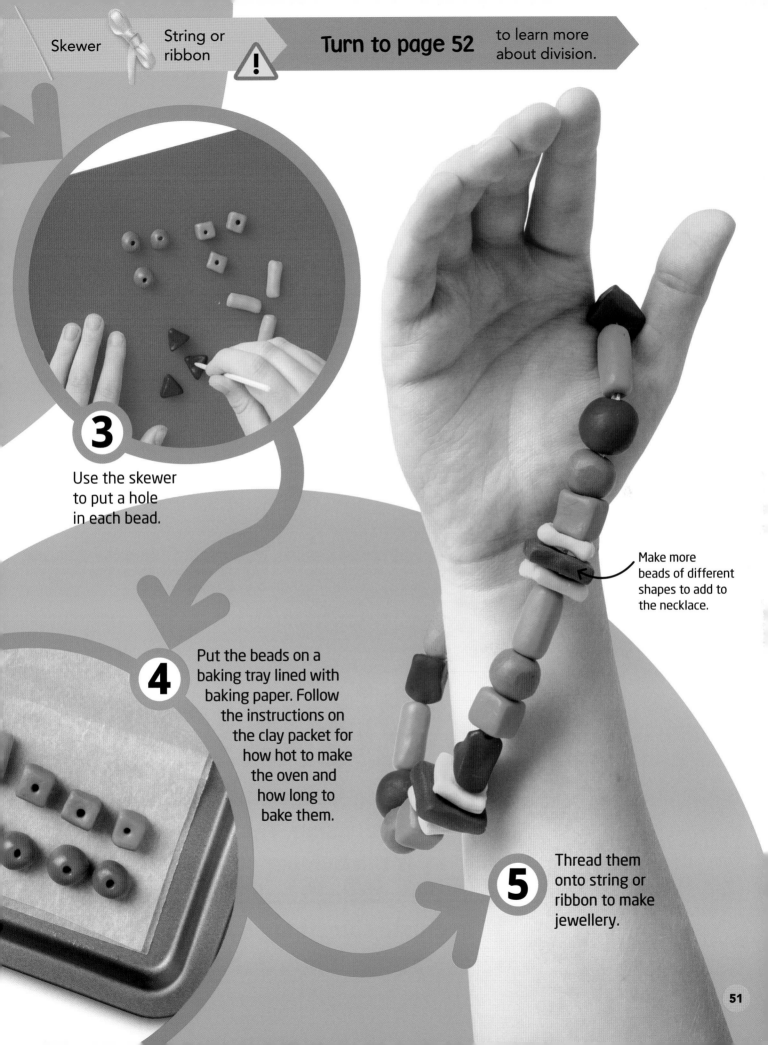

3 Use the skewer to put a hole in each bead.

4 Put the beads on a baking tray lined with baking paper. Follow the instructions on the clay packet for how hot to make the oven and how long to bake them.

Make more beads of different shapes to add to the necklace.

5 Thread them onto string or ribbon to make jewellery.

Repeated subtraction

Division is like subtracting the same amount many times. Let's try an example: 12 divided by 3. You start by subtracting the second number in the sum from the first...

$$12 \div 3$$

12 − 3 = 9

Removing 3 marbles from 12 marbles leaves 9.

9 − 3 = 6

Removing 3 marbles from 9 marbles leaves 6.

6 − 3 = 3

Removing 3 marbles from 6 marbles leaves 3.

3 − 3 = 0

Removing 3 marbles from 3 marbles leaves none!

The number of times you subtracted is the answer to the sum.

$$12 \div 3 = 4$$

Dividing things up

You can divide a group of items up between people by giving one item to each person in turn, until all the items are gone. If there are 56 toys to share out between seven classes at playtime and the classes take one each until the toys are gone, each class ends up with eight toys.

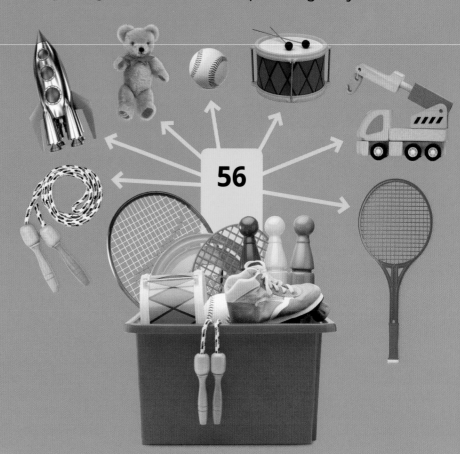

56

Division

Splitting things into equal amounts is called division. The number you divide by is the number of equal parts you are splitting something into. So if you divide something by three, you're breaking it into three equal amounts.

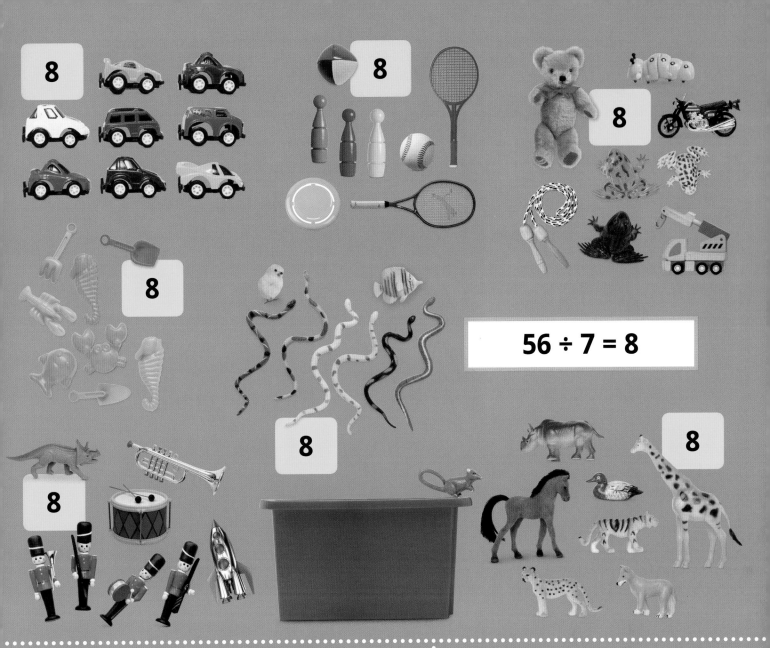

8 **8** **8**

8

$$56 \div 7 = 8$$

8 **8**

8

Division vs. multiplication

Division is the opposite of multiplication. If two numbers multiply to give another, then that number divided by each of the other numbers will give you the leftover number in the sum. We call such numbers opposite operators.

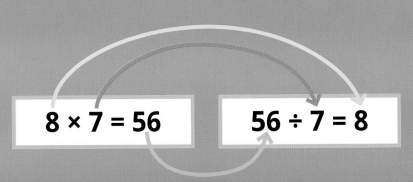

$$8 \times 7 = 56$$

$$56 \div 7 = 8$$

Can you guess the answer to 56 divided by 8?

Dividing by one

You can already divide by one, because any number divided by one is itself! It's the same as saying you want to share 10 balls with yourself - you get all 10. What's the biggest number you can think of? Divide it by one - you get the same again.

$$10 \div 1 = 10$$

Symmetry

Arrays

Architecture

Times tables

Engineering

Nets

Angles

Prisms

Out and about

Next time you leave your home, look around with a mathematician's eye. You might notice an unusually shaped building or a symmetrical leaf. Natural objects can also inspire crafts that help you remember maths facts.

Buildings

From your own home to churches and museums, buildings of all shapes and sizes are everywhere you look. Architects, who come up with ideas for buildings, use measurements and shapes to design them. Maths is also what holds a building up! The strength and size of each part has to be worked out.

Around the world

The shape of a building or bridge can be linked to a place or a period in history. Ancient Roman buildings often feature arches. Religious buildings can also have distinct shapes. Christian churches often sport pointed cones called spires, and Muslim mosques can have towers called minarets.

Look for shapes

Buildings can have many different-shaped parts. Roofs are often triangular to help rain run off them. Rectangular bricks fit together without any holes between them. What shapes does your home have?

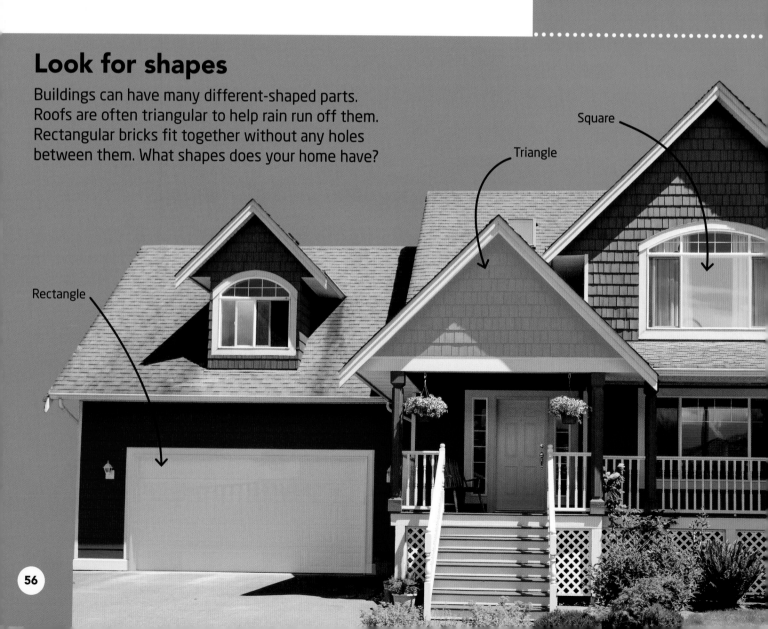

Square

Triangle

Rectangle

Pont du Gard, France

Hagia Sophia, Turkey

Measurements

We use measurements to make sure things are the correct size. When planning buildings, measurements must be done very carefully, with no mistakes. If you use the wrong measurement then a door might not fit in its frame, and there could be gaps between walls!

Architecture

Architects use their imagination to dream up new buildings. They think about what the building will be used for, and how it will fit into the surrounding area. They create detailed drawings to show the building's lines and angles, along with each measurement. Engineers use this plan to make the building.

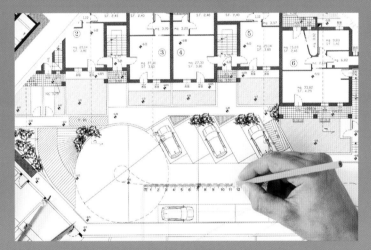
Architectural drawings

Building plans are carefully checked.

Engineering

Turning a drawing into reality is a big task. Engineers use maths to turn plans into buildings. The calculations they have to do along the way include finding the amount of material they'll need to build the walls. They also need to make strong foundations underneath the building that will hold it up.

Zaha Hadid

Architect and designer • 1950–2016 • From Iraq

Zaha Hadid created fantastic-shaped buildings and structures in many different countries. Her designs included lots of curves and round shapes. She became one of the most well-known architects in the world and won lots of awards for her work.

Heydar Aliyev Center

In 2007, Zaha designed this curved creation in Azerbaijan. It took five years to complete and contains a gallery, museum, and huge event spaces. The rounded lines often used by Zaha make her buildings stand out. She based some of the curved lines in her work on the way that water flows.

Architects and buildings

Architects think about what the building will be used for as well as how to make it look good. Many of Zaha's ideas and projects were unique and eye-catching, so she was asked to design important buildings, such as the centre that housed the swimming pool for the London 2012 Olympic Games in London, UK.

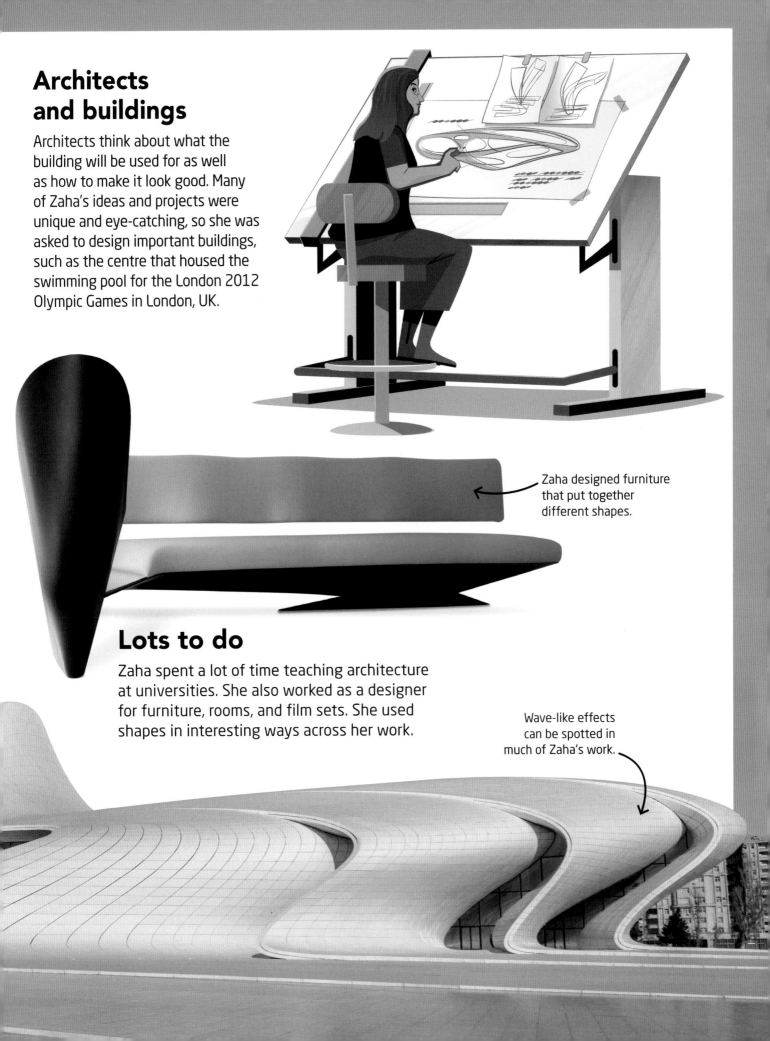

Zaha designed furniture that put together different shapes.

Lots to do

Zaha spent a lot of time teaching architecture at universities. She also worked as a designer for furniture, rooms, and film sets. She used shapes in interesting ways across her work.

Wave-like effects can be spotted in much of Zaha's work.

Shape city

Imagine a 3D shape unfolding into a flat shape. This is called the shape's net. Use the nets on pages 62–65 to make building blocks for your own city. You could make all the differently shaped buildings you see in a real city - including homes, schools, museums, and much more!

1

Trace a net from the following pages onto card and carefully cut it out with scissors.

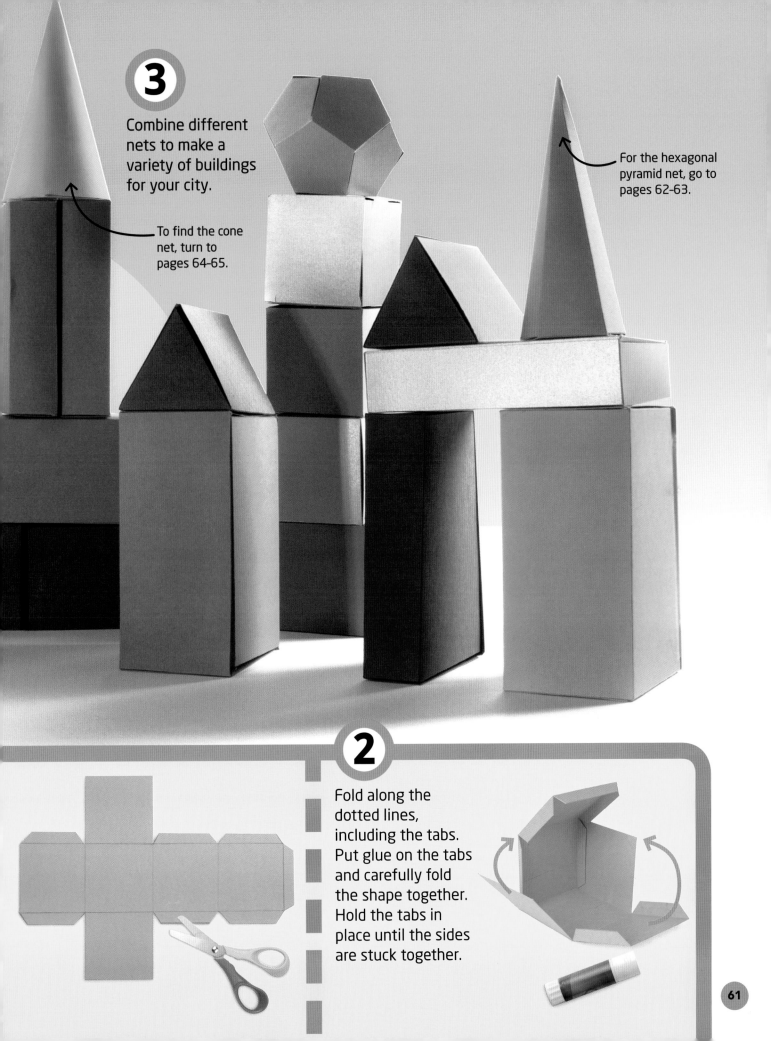

3

Combine different nets to make a variety of buildings for your city.

To find the cone net, turn to pages 64–65.

For the hexagonal pyramid net, go to pages 62–63.

2

Fold along the dotted lines, including the tabs. Put glue on the tabs and carefully fold the shape together. Hold the tabs in place until the sides are stuck together.

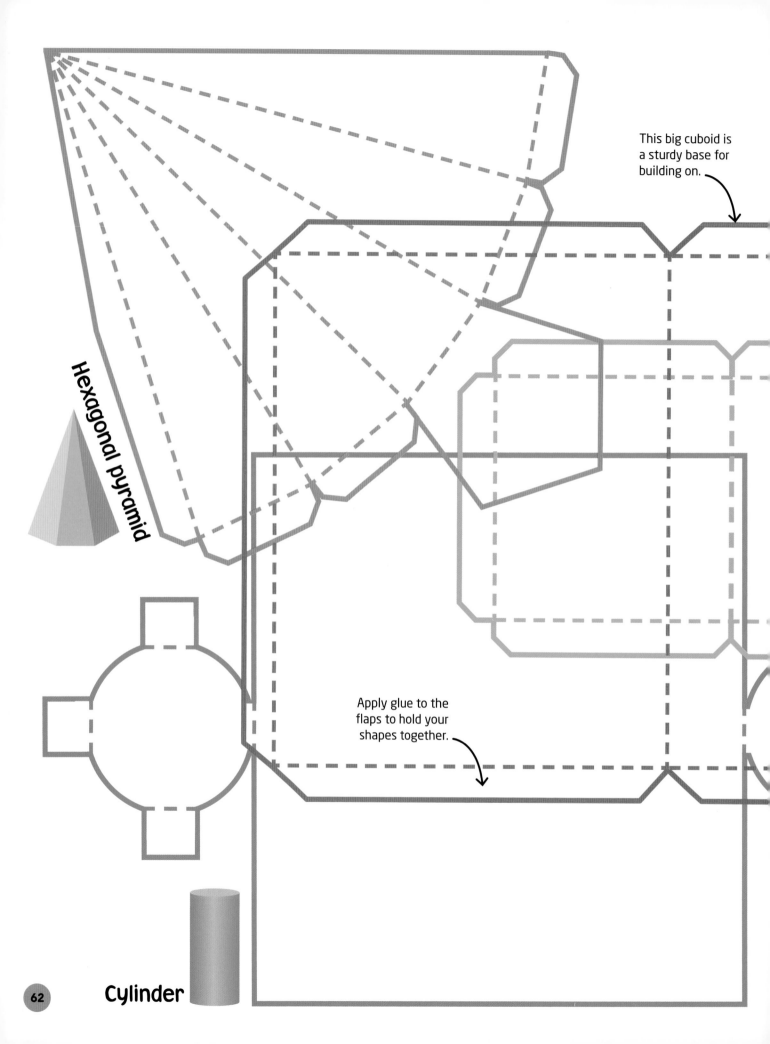

This big cuboid is a sturdy base for building on.

Hexagonal pyramid

Apply glue to the flaps to hold your shapes together.

Cylinder

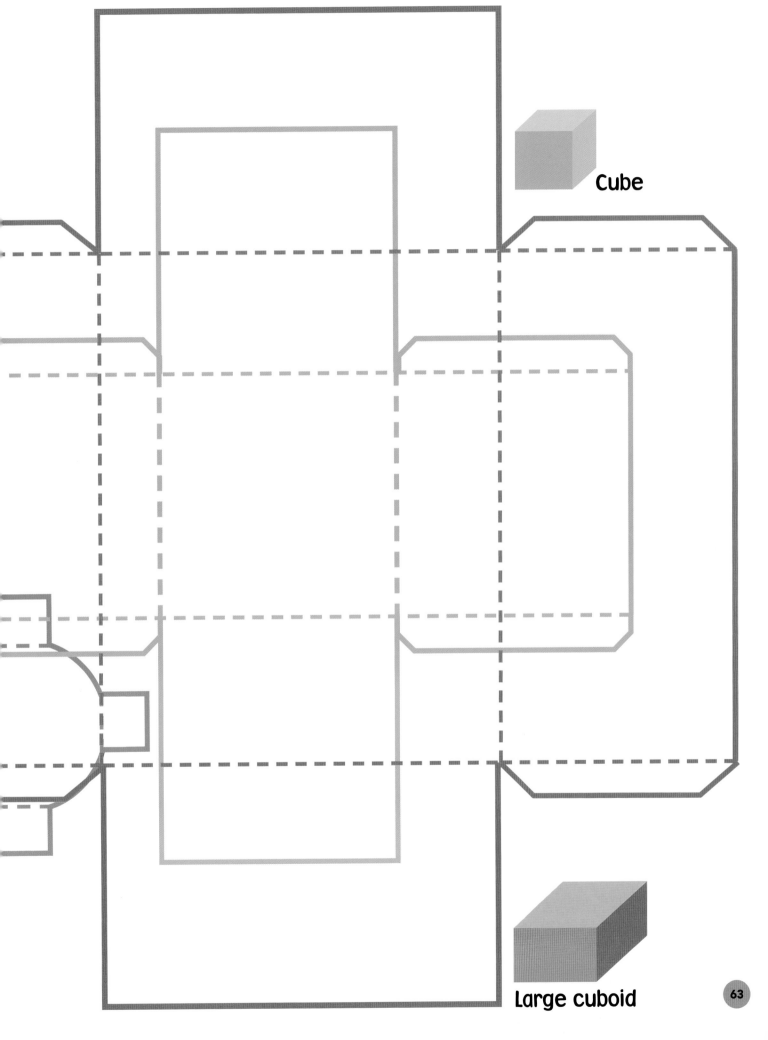

Cube

Large cuboid

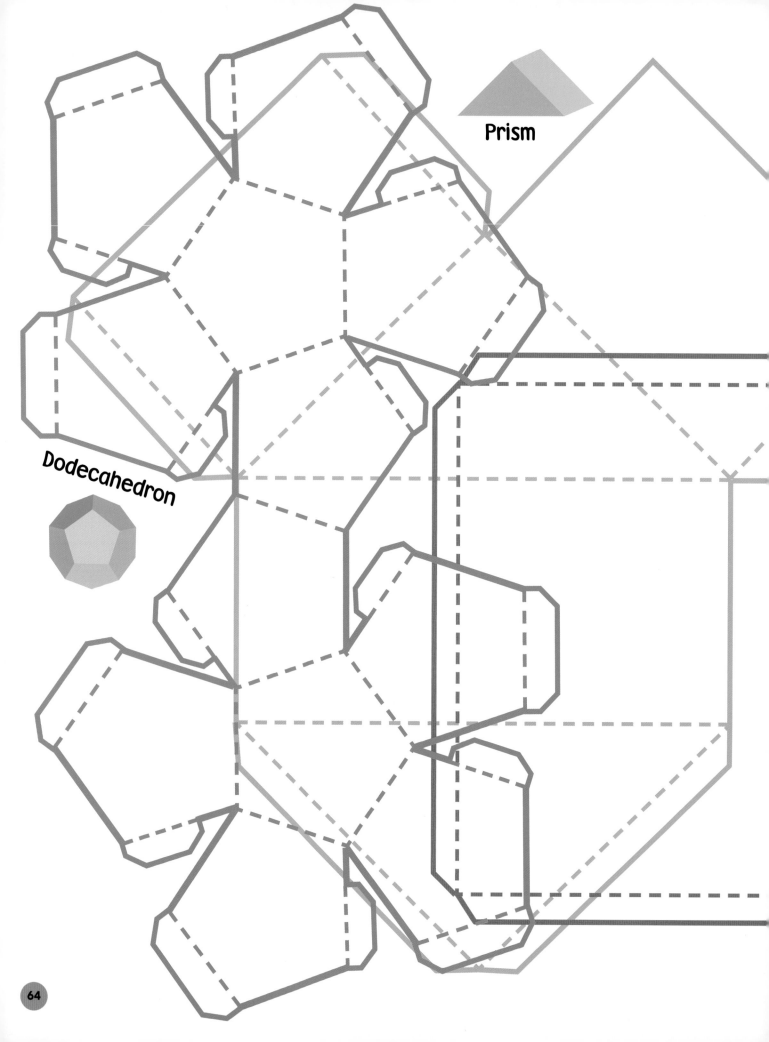

Prism

Dodecahedron

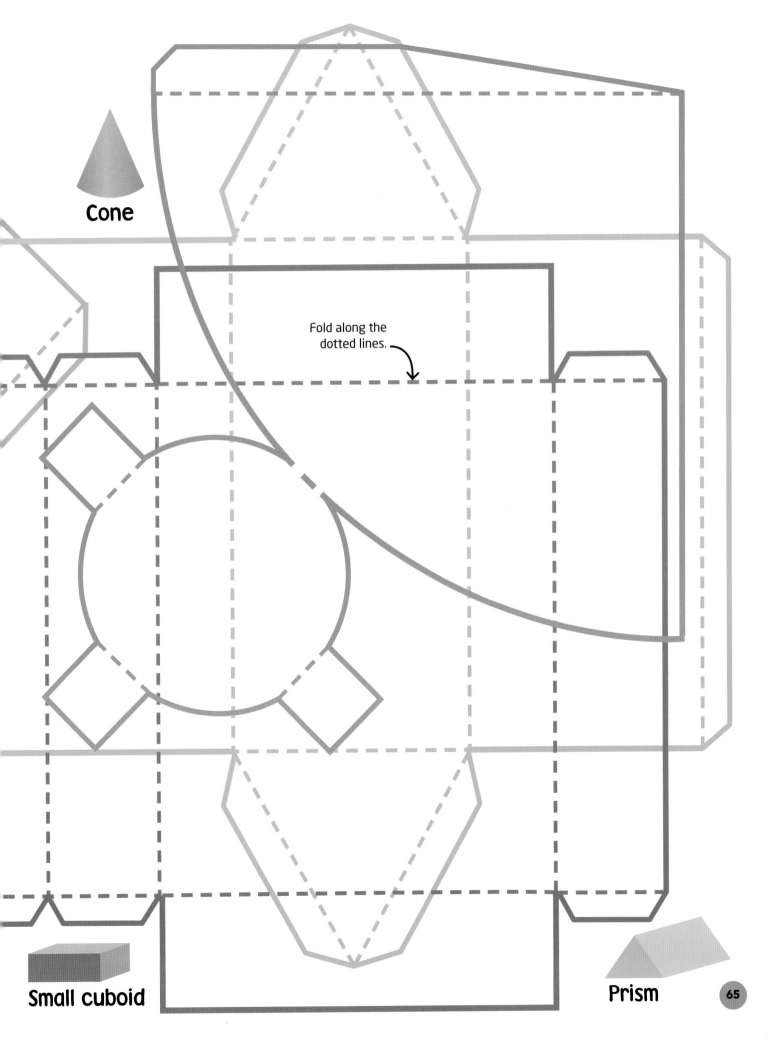

Cone

Fold along the
dotted lines.

Small cuboid

Prism

You will need

Paper

Scissors

Glue stick

Möbius loop

A mobius loop is a shape with only one side and one edge. Follow the steps on these pages to make a paper version. Trace your finger along the single side - it goes on forever!

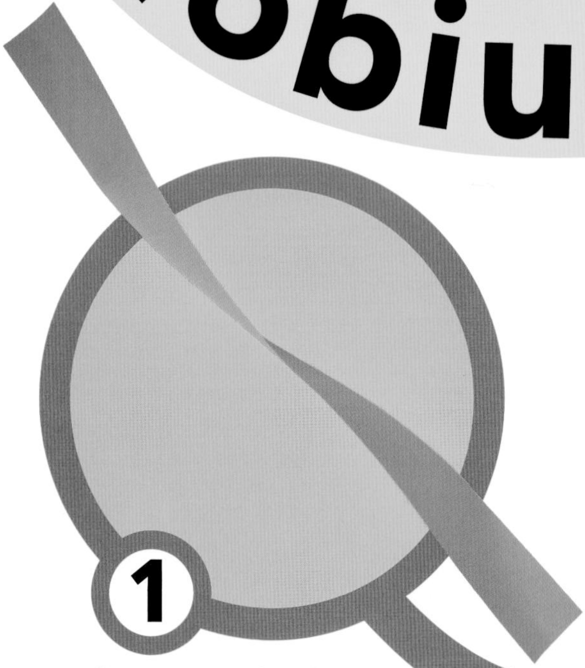

1

Cut out a strip of paper. Do a half-twist like the one above.

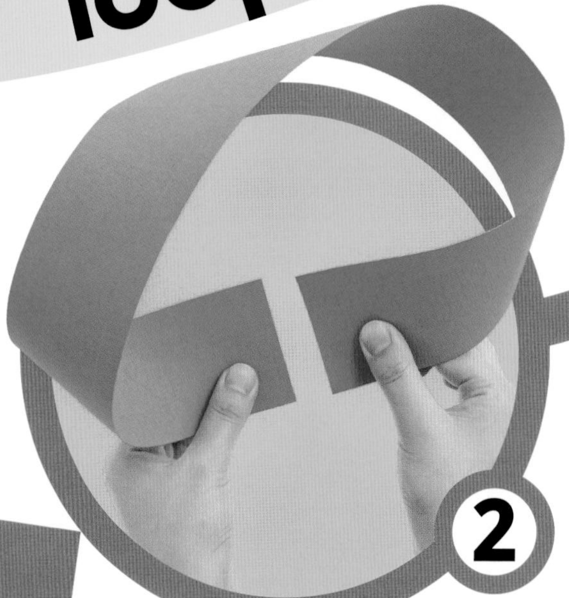

2

Keeping it twisted, use the glue to stick the ends together.

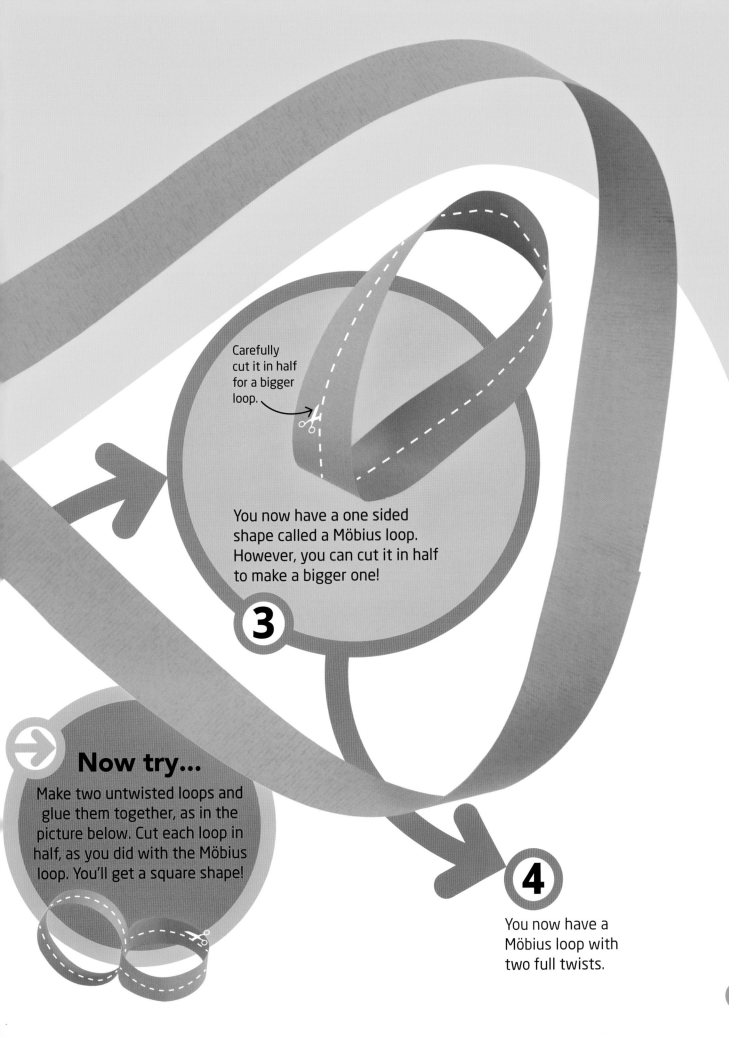

Carefully cut it in half for a bigger loop.

You now have a one sided shape called a Möbius loop. However, you can cut it in half to make a bigger one!

3

Now try...

Make two untwisted loops and glue them together, as in the picture below. Cut each loop in half, as you did with the Möbius loop. You'll get a square shape!

4

You now have a Möbius loop with two full twists.

You will need
A narrow, see-through cuboid container
A wide, see-through cuboid container
A ruler

Rainwater measures

We usually measure rainfall in centimetres (cm) or inches (in). Find out how much rain falls in your area during the next month with this experiment. Then, find out the volume of the rainwater you've collected. You could use it to water plants!

1 Place the containers outside your home. Make sure they're not under shelter, as this will stop rain from reaching them.

The containers need to be cuboid in shape.

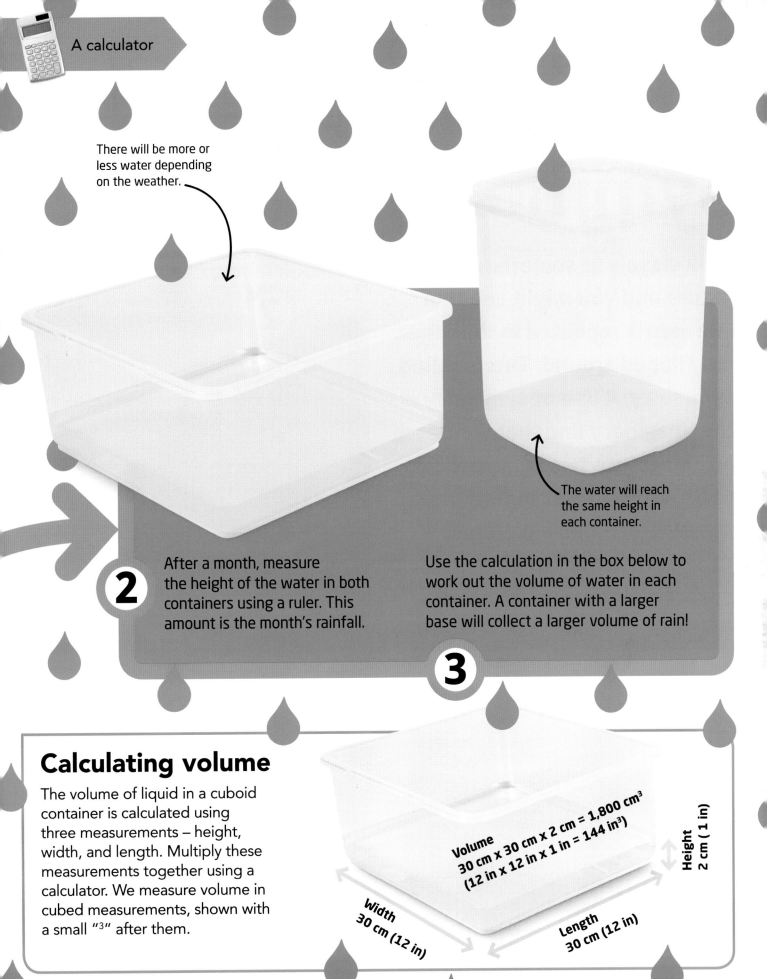

A calculator

There will be more or less water depending on the weather.

The water will reach the same height in each container.

2 After a month, measure the height of the water in both containers using a ruler. This amount is the month's rainfall.

3 Use the calculation in the box below to work out the volume of water in each container. A container with a larger base will collect a larger volume of rain!

Calculating volume

The volume of liquid in a cuboid container is calculated using three measurements – height, width, and length. Multiply these measurements together using a calculator. We measure volume in cubed measurements, shown with a small "³" after them.

Volume
30 cm x 30 cm x 2 cm = 1,800 cm³
(12 in x 12 in x 1 in = 144 in³)

Height
2 cm (1 in)

Width
30 cm (12 in)

Length
30 cm (12 in)

Natural symmetry

Look closely at something in nature and you might see that one side is repeated in the other, but flipped around. This is called symmetry. A line of symmetry is the imaginary line that divides an object into two symmetrical parts. Use a mirror to find symmetry in these pictures.

Faces

Your face might look symmetrical, but it probably isn't! Use a mirror to check out the unique features on each side of your face.

1

You can use a mirror to find out if an object has a line of symmetry by seeing if the reflection looks like the opposite side. If this only happens once, it has one line of symmetry.

This butterfly has one line of symmetry.

2

Objects can have more than one line of symmetry. Hold the mirror along each of the dotted lines on these pictures. How many lines of symmetry do they have?

This flower has four lines of symmetry.

Original face

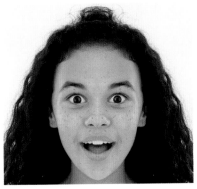

Left symmetry

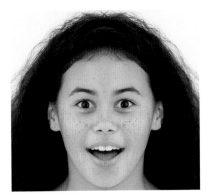

Right symmetry

This clover has three lines of symmetry.

Now try...

Collect your own objects and test to see how many lines of symmetry they have. Are there particular types of flower or plant that have more than one line of symmetry?

3

Some objects don't have sides that repeat in the same way as symmetrical items. This means there are no lines of symmetry. The patterns on either side are unique!

Hold the mirror on this shell to see how the reflections look different.

Rotating
starfish

Rotate this book and you can see it change position. However, some shapes look the same when they're rotated. They have what we call "rotational symmetry". The number of positions in which a shape looks the same are called its order of rotational symmetry.

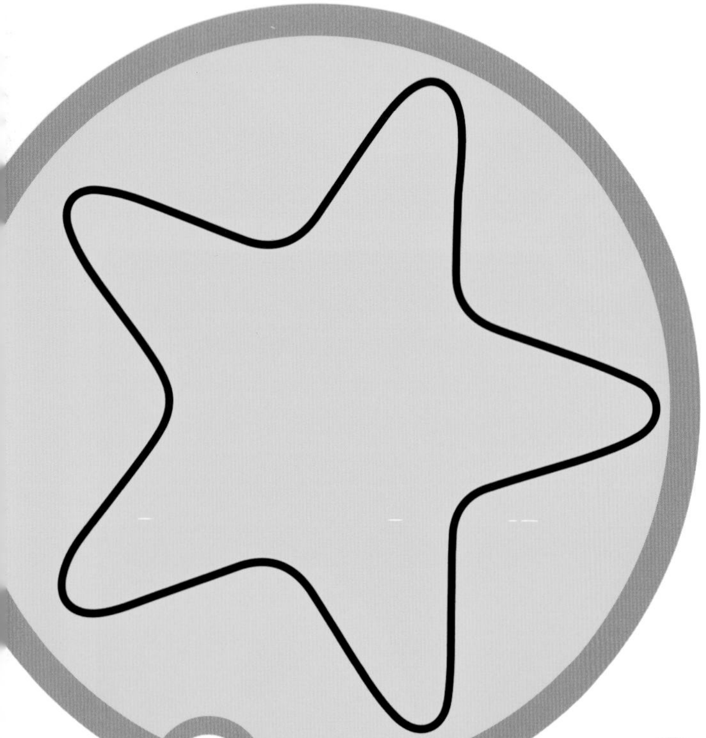

2

Cut the starfish outline out of the pink paper and decorate it. Add an arrow on one of the legs.

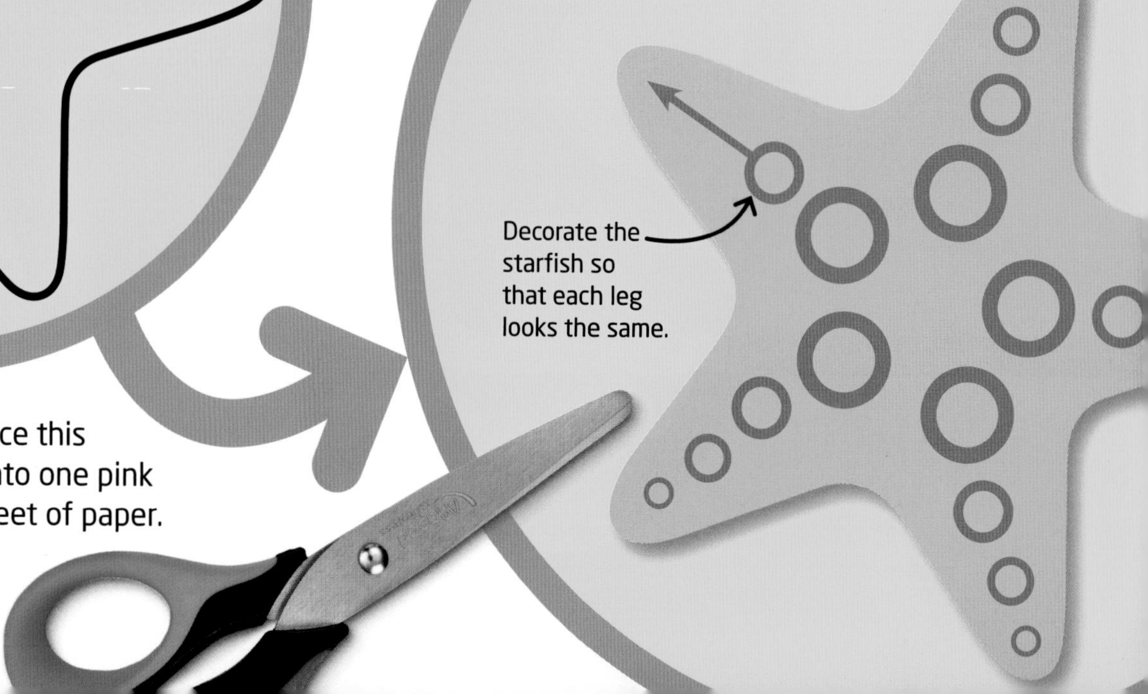

Decorate the starfish so that each leg looks the same.

1

Use a pencil to trace this starfish outline onto one pink and one white sheet of paper.

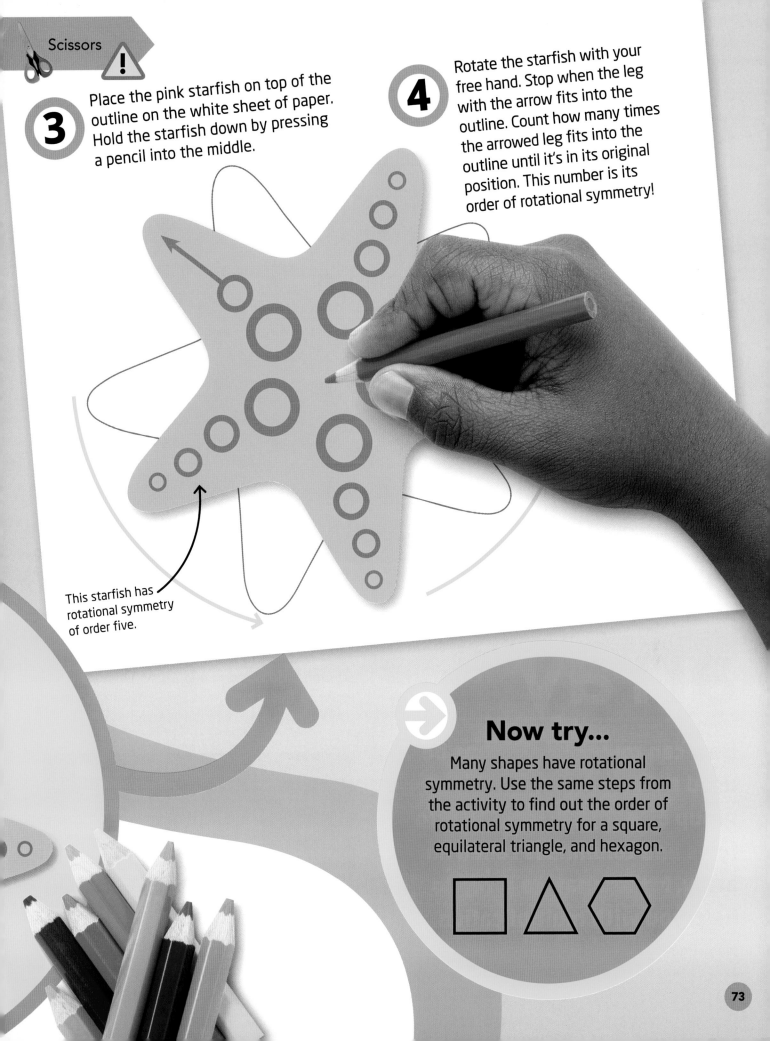

Scissors !

3 Place the pink starfish on top of the outline on the white sheet of paper. Hold the starfish down by pressing a pencil into the middle.

4 Rotate the starfish with your free hand. Stop when the leg with the arrow fits into the outline. Count how many times the arrowed leg fits into the outline until it's in its original position. This number is its order of rotational symmetry!

This starfish has rotational symmetry of order five.

Now try...

Many shapes have rotational symmetry. Use the same steps from the activity to find out the order of rotational symmetry for a square, equilateral triangle, and hexagon.

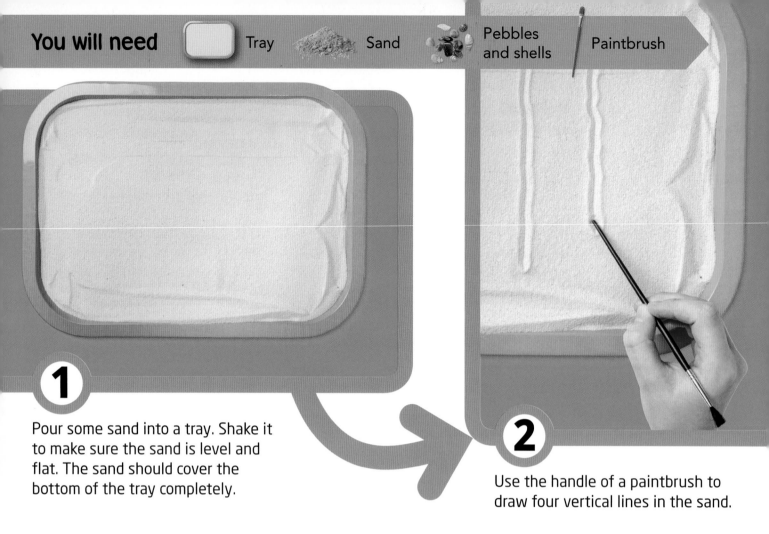

1

Pour some sand into a tray. Shake it to make sure the sand is level and flat. The sand should cover the bottom of the tray completely.

2

Use the handle of a paintbrush to draw four vertical lines in the sand.

Nature array

How can rows and columns be used to do multiplication? A group of things organised into rows and columns is called an array. Make a nature array to help you with multiplication.

Array multiplication

We can use the rows and columns in an array to work out multiplication sums. In the array below, there are five trays in each column, and three in each row. This is the same as five trays times three. Counting the trays gives us 15, which means 5 x 3 = 15.

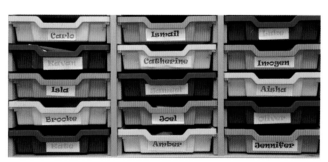

There is a book in the tray in the third column on the second row. Having the trays in an array allows us to describe how to find them more easily.

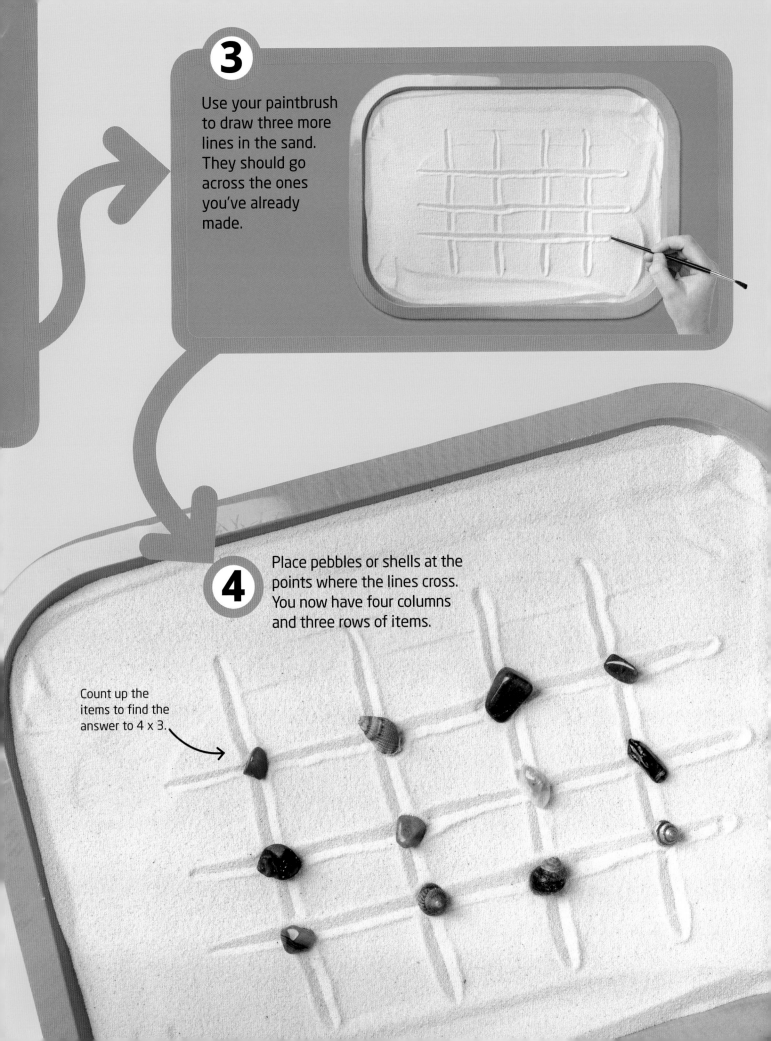

3 Use your paintbrush to draw three more lines in the sand. They should go across the ones you've already made.

4 Place pebbles or shells at the points where the lines cross. You now have four columns and three rows of items.

Count up the items to find the answer to 4 x 3.

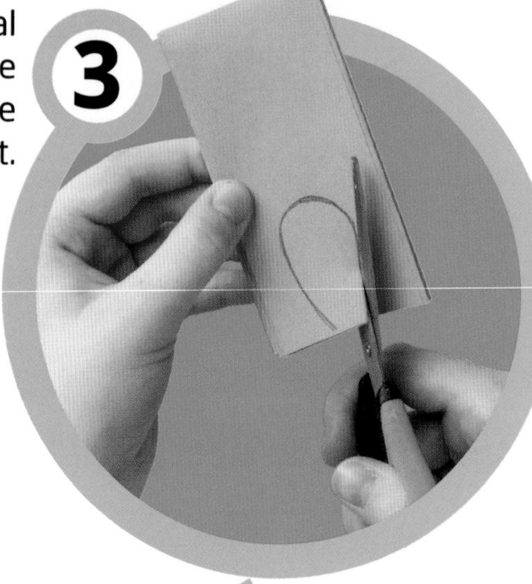

3 Draw a petal shape at the unfolded edge and cut it out.

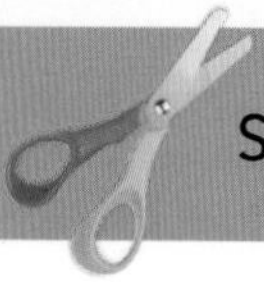

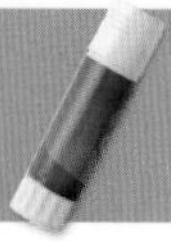

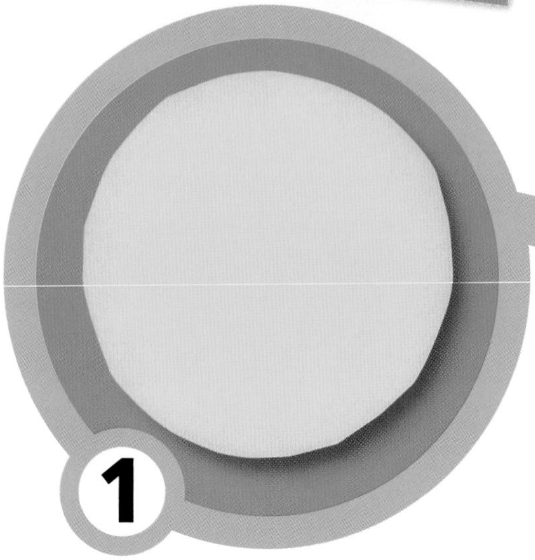

1 Cut out a circle of yellow paper to be the centre of your flower.

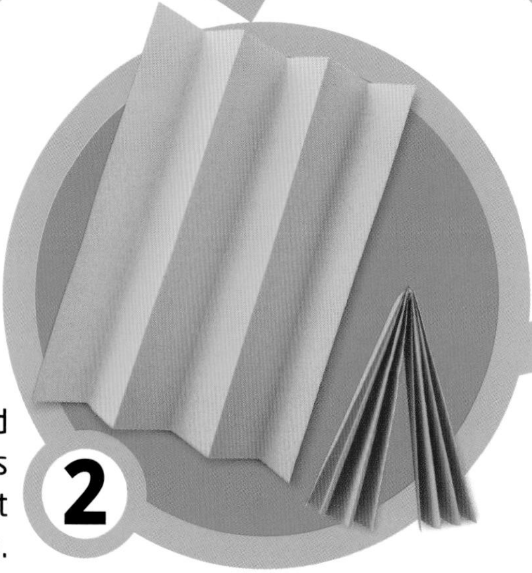

2 Fold a different coloured sheet of paper five times lengthways. Then, fold it in half, top to bottom.

Times-table flowers

These mathematical flowers will help you remember your times tables. Have fun making them for each number, and you'll end up with a lovely bunch of multiplication flowers to decorate your room.

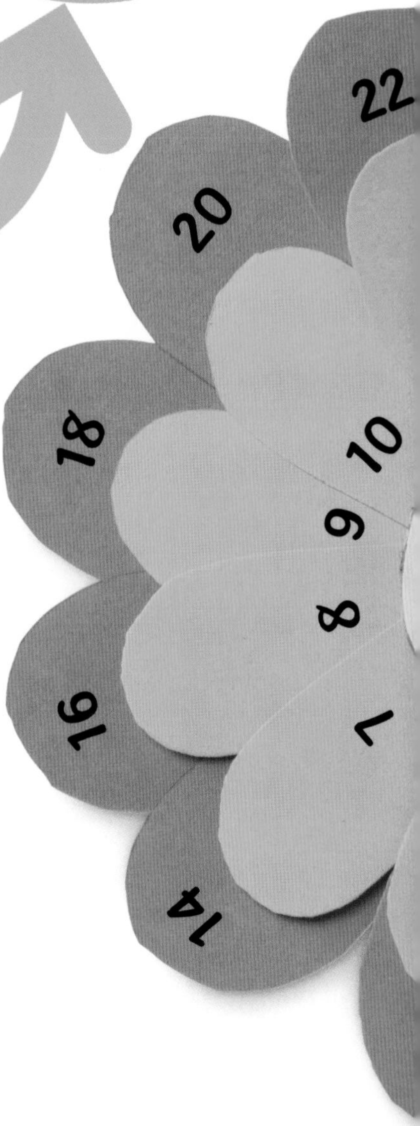

22 20 18 16 14 7 8 9 10

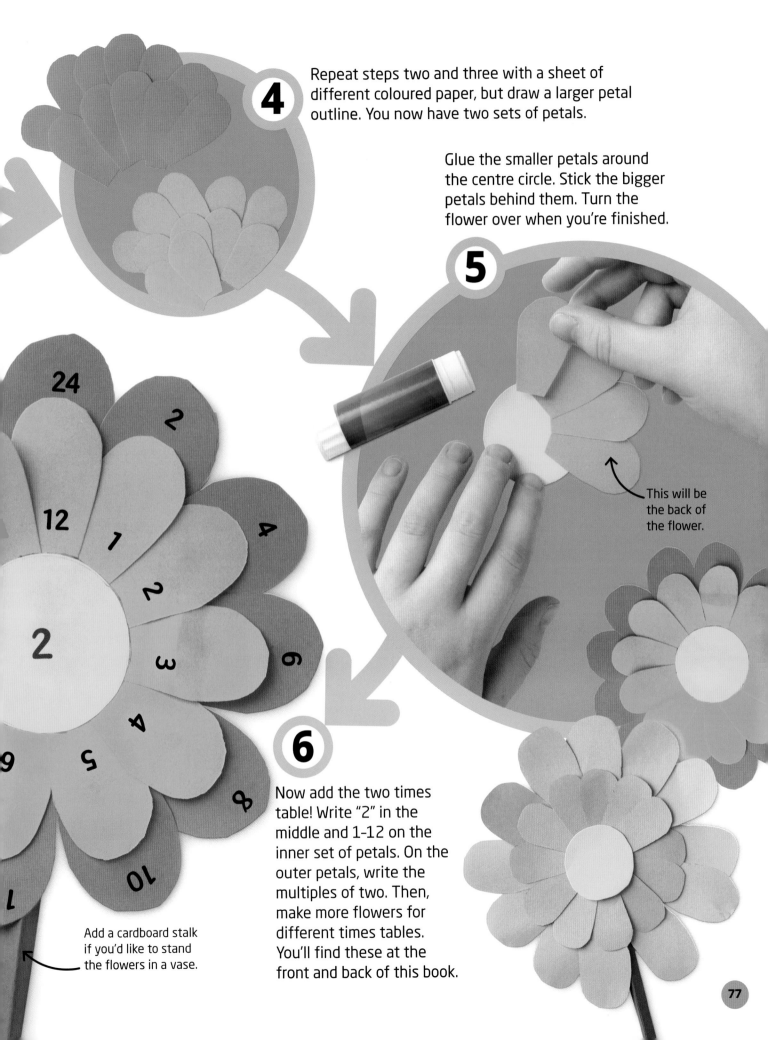

4 Repeat steps two and three with a sheet of different coloured paper, but draw a larger petal outline. You now have two sets of petals.

Glue the smaller petals around the centre circle. Stick the bigger petals behind them. Turn the flower over when you're finished.

5

This will be the back of the flower.

24

2

12

1

4

2

3

6

2

4

5

8

6

10

1

Add a cardboard stalk if you'd like to stand the flowers in a vase.

6 Now add the two times table! Write "2" in the middle and 1–12 on the inner set of petals. On the outer petals, write the multiples of two. Then, make more flowers for different times tables. You'll find these at the front and back of this book.

Decimals

Clocks

Speed

Getting around

Every time you plan a journey, you're using maths. You need to know the distance you're travelling, how long it will take to get there, and how fast you'll need to go to arrive on time!

Minutes

There are 60 seconds in a minute. You might use minutes to measure the length of a TV show, or a short walk within your neighbourhood. How many minutes does it take to get home from your local park?

Seconds

This is one of the smallest lengths of time. Can you say the word "alligator", "battleship", or "Mississippi"? It takes roughly one second to say each of these words. You probably count in seconds when you play hide-and-seek.

Minute line

Hour line

The large hand moves between the minute lines to show a minute passing.

Some clocks have an extra, skinnier hand that ticks forward once a second.

11   1

10

9

8   7   6

Time

Time is the measurement of how long it takes for things to happen. We measure time in all sorts of units, from tiny seconds to long years. Take a few minutes to read all about time across the next four pages.

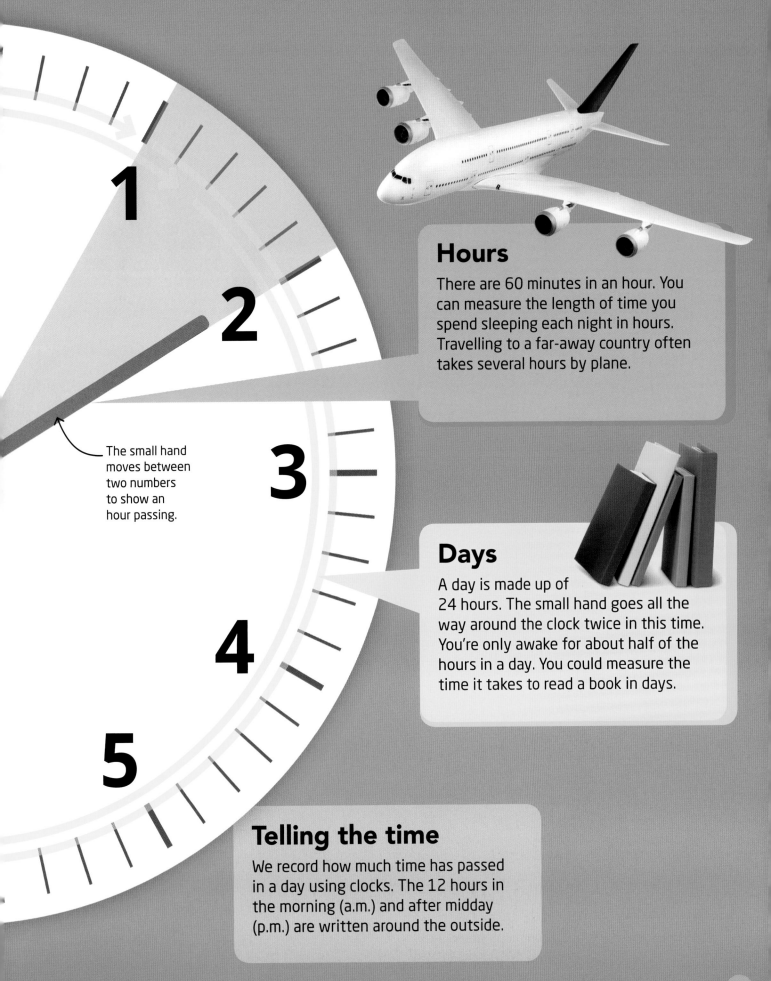

1

2

The small hand moves between two numbers to show an hour passing.

3

4

5

Hours

There are 60 minutes in an hour. You can measure the length of time you spend sleeping each night in hours. Travelling to a far-away country often takes several hours by plane.

Days

A day is made up of 24 hours. The small hand goes all the way around the clock twice in this time. You're only awake for about half of the hours in a day. You could measure the time it takes to read a book in days.

Telling the time

We record how much time has passed in a day using clocks. The 12 hours in the morning (a.m.) and after midday (p.m.) are written around the outside.

Before clocks were invented, some people used the position of the Sun in the sky to tell the time.

The 24 hours of the day start at midnight. This is shown as 00:00 on a 24-hour clock.

00:00

Digital time

Phones and computer screens show digital clocks. These present the time as numbers. The hour is written first, followed by a colon (:), and then the minutes past the hour.

This digital clock shows 52 minutes past nine.

12:00

11:00

10:00

00:00

23:00

22:00

21:00

The day's last hour is 23:00, (11 p.m.).

09:00

20:00

On a 24-hour clock eight o'clock would be 08:00 in the morning, or 20:00 in the evening.

08:00

19:00

18:00

Sunset

07:00

12-hour or 24-hour?

Some people use a 24-hour clock to tell the time. Rather than having a.m. and p.m. times, these clocks count every hour in the day.

06:00

01:00

13:00

02:00

14:00

15:00

03:00

16:00

04:00

00

05:00

Sunrise

Days, weeks, and months

There are seven days in a week. Months are 28, 29, 30, or 31 days long. We record longer passages of time on a calendar.

One calendar page shows a month.

Each column has a day of the week at the top. The dates in one column all fall on that day.

October

Sunday	Monday	Tuesday	Wednesday	Thursday	Friday	Saturday
				1	2	3
4	5	6	7	8	9	10
11	12	13	14	15	16	17
18	19	20	21	22	23	24
25	26	27	28	29	30	31

Each day in a month has a number called a date.

People celebrate becoming a year older on their birthday.

Years

A year is 12 months long. This is the time it takes for the Earth to go all the way around the Sun. We measure our age in years – how old are you?

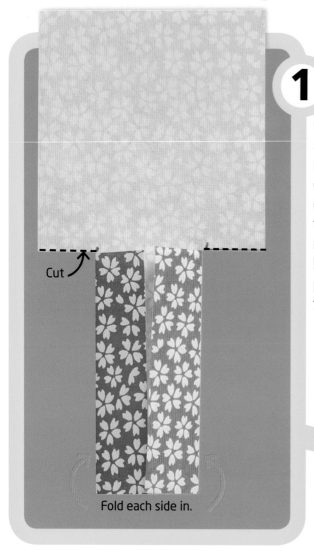

1 Cut out a rectangle of paper. Half way down, make two cuts a quarter of the way into the rectangle. Fold in both sides of the paper below the cuts.

Cut

Fold each side in.

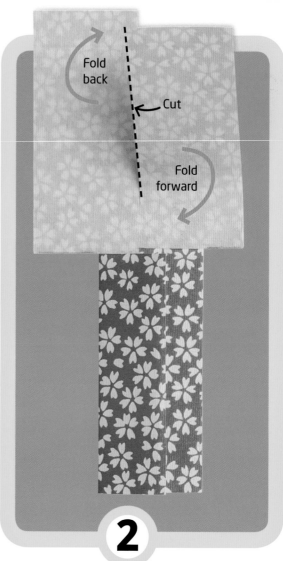

Fold back

Cut

Fold forward

2 To make two wings, cut downwards from the top in the middle, to one third of the way down (as shown). Fold the wings in opposite directions. Add a paperclip to the bottom for weight.

Timing helicopters

Does it take longer for something heavy or light to reach the ground? We can measure time to work this out. We also need things to drop...

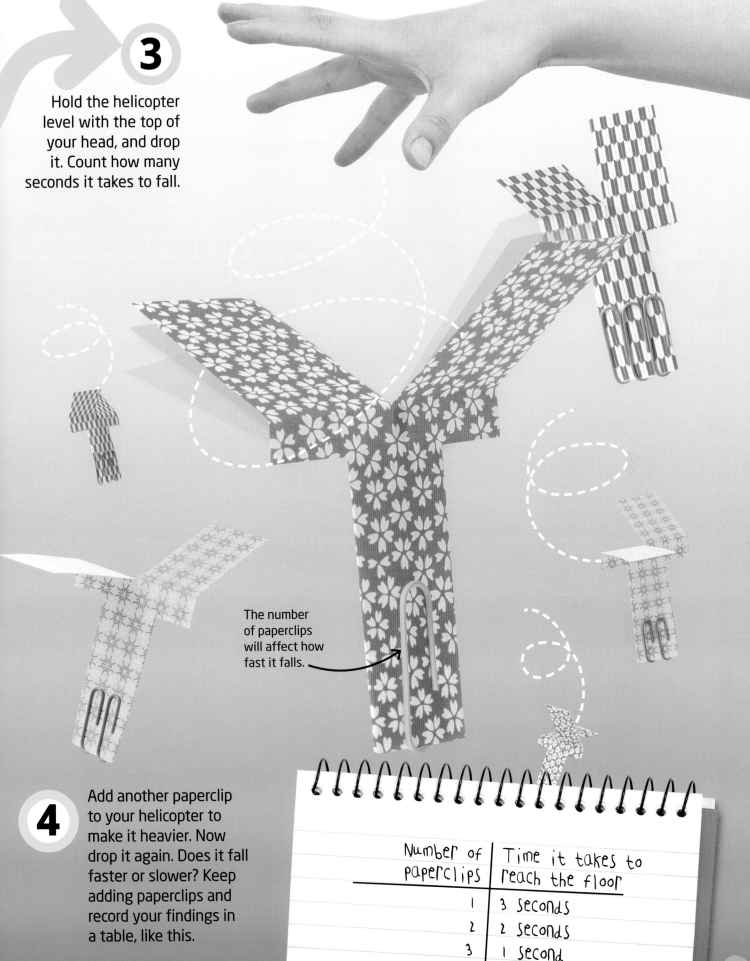

3

Hold the helicopter level with the top of your head, and drop it. Count how many seconds it takes to fall.

The number of paperclips will affect how fast it falls.

4

Add another paperclip to your helicopter to make it heavier. Now drop it again. Does it fall faster or slower? Keep adding paperclips and record your findings in a table, like this.

Number of paperclips	Time it takes to reach the floor
1	3 seconds
2	2 seconds
3	1 second

Let's learn how to measure distance using a high-speed competition between toy cars. Gather some friends, pick your cars, and follow the steps on these pages. The one that goes the furthest wins!

Distance competition

2 Hold your cars at the top and let them go at the same time.

3 Wait for the cars to come to a standstill. Then, measure how far they travelled using a piece of string.

Hold the string at the front of the car.

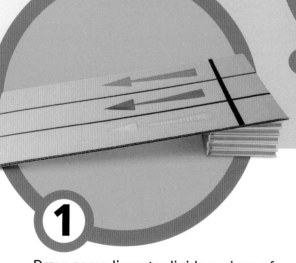

1 Draw some lines to divide a piece of cardboard into lanes. Add a starting line across the top. Then, prop it up on a pile of books to make a ramp.

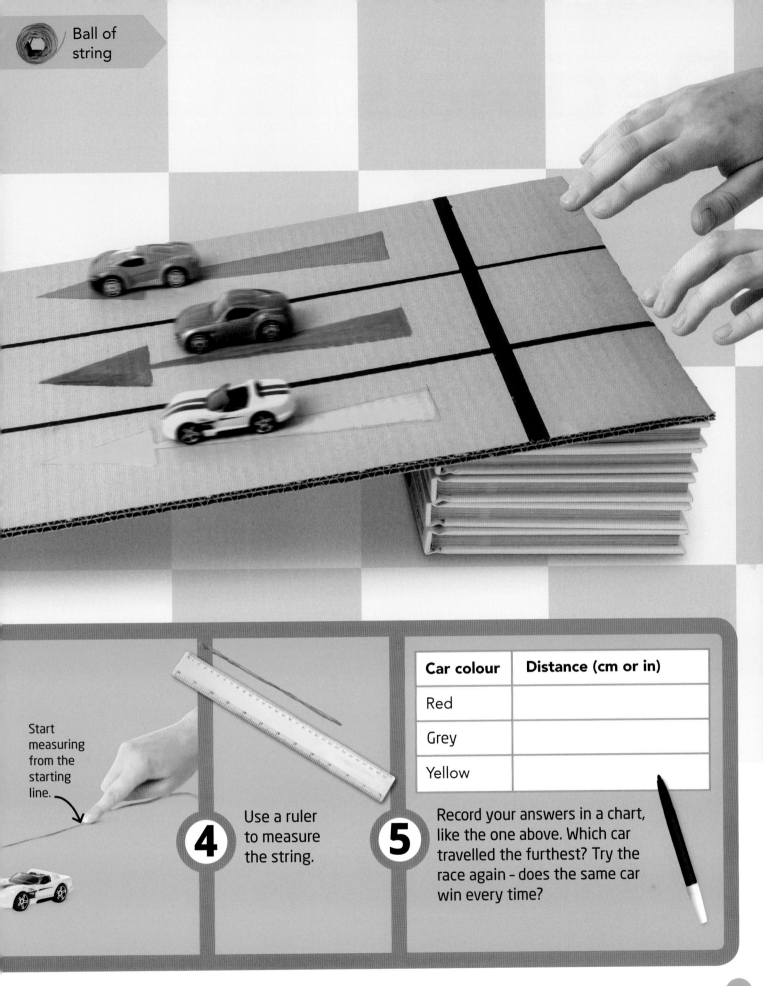

Ball of string

Car colour	Distance (cm or in)
Red	
Grey	
Yellow	

Start measuring from the starting line.

4 Use a ruler to measure the string.

5 Record your answers in a chart, like the one above. Which car travelled the furthest? Try the race again - does the same car win every time?

Decimals

Decimals are a way of showing numbers smaller than one. We write them after a decimal point, which looks just like a full stop.

The decimal point

Any number that comes after a decimal point is smaller than one. This is called a decimal number. The further away a digit is from the point, the smaller it is. Everything to the left of the point is a whole number.

Decimal point

1.25

Whole numbers ← → Decimal numbers

Tenths, hundredths, and thousandths

If you divide one by 10, you get one tenth, which is written as 0.1 as a decimal. Dividing one by 100 gives you one hundredth, or 0.01, and dividing it by 1,000 gives you one thousandth, or 0.001.

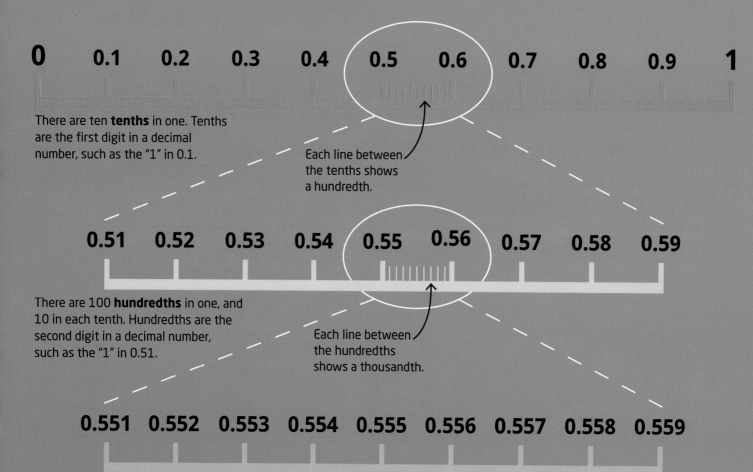

0 0.1 0.2 0.3 0.4 0.5 0.6 0.7 0.8 0.9 1

There are ten **tenths** in one. Tenths are the first digit in a decimal number, such as the "1" in 0.1.

Each line between the tenths shows a hundredth.

0.51 0.52 0.53 0.54 0.55 0.56 0.57 0.58 0.59

There are 100 **hundredths** in one, and 10 in each tenth. Hundredths are the second digit in a decimal number, such as the "1" in 0.51.

Each line between the hundredths shows a thousandth.

0.551 0.552 0.553 0.554 0.555 0.556 0.557 0.558 0.559

There are 1,000 **thousandths** in one, and 10 in each hundredth. Thousandths are the third digit in a decimal number, such as the "1" in 0.551.

Money

We often use decimals in real life when we use money to buy or sell things. Many currencies (types of money) are whole amounts and decimals.

Each penny (p) is one hundredth of a pound (£).

= **£2.45**

Time

Sometimes we need to measure time very precisely, for example to find out who won a very close race. Tiny fractions of time are shown as decimals on stopwatches.

Whole seconds are shown on the left of the decimal point.

This is a tenth of a second.

This is a hundredth of a second.

This is a thousandth of a second!

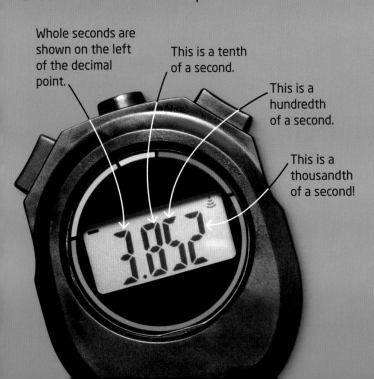

Decimals and fractions

Fractions are another way to write numbers smaller than one. Any decimal can also be written as a fraction, and vice versa. To get the decimal version of a fraction, use a calculator to divide the top number by the bottom number.

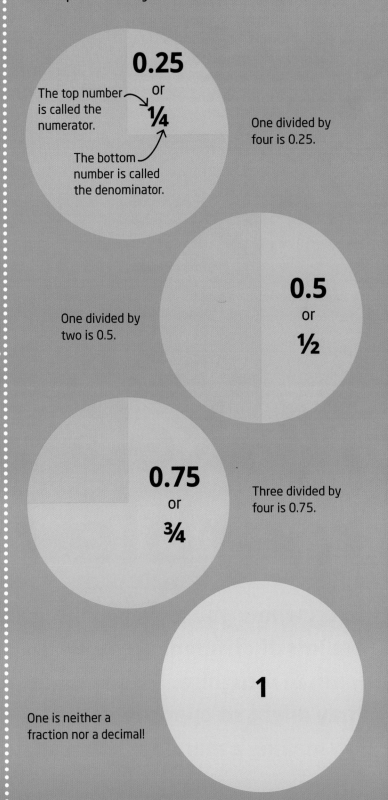

0.25
or
¼

The top number is called the numerator.

The bottom number is called the denominator.

One divided by four is 0.25.

0.5
or
½

One divided by two is 0.5.

0.75
or
¾

Three divided by four is 0.75.

1

One is neither a fraction nor a decimal!

 Cardboard box

 Glue stick

 Scissors

 Marbles

Line types

Different types of line include horizontal (running left to right), vertical (running top to bottom), and diagonal (running on a slant). These can be perpendicular (meeting one another) or parallel (running alongside one another).

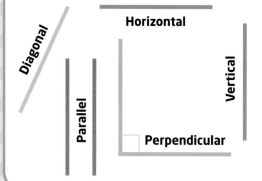

Diagonal

Horizontal

Vertical

Parallel

Perpendicular

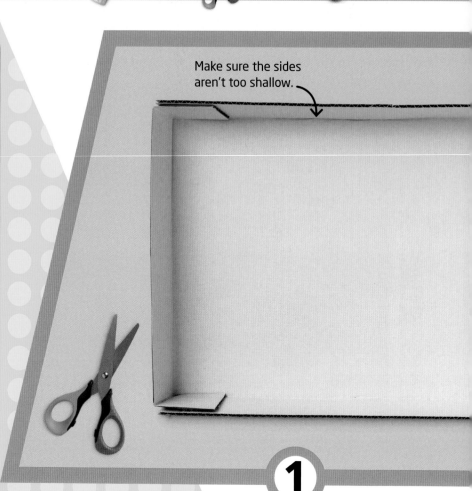

Make sure the sides aren't too shallow.

1

Cut a cardboard box down to about 3 cm (1 in) thick.

Make a marble run

Everywhere you look, you'll see lines. There are lots of different types, which you'll soon learn to recognise. These interact in different ways – they might sit opposite each other or form a corner. Try making a marble run that shows off them all!

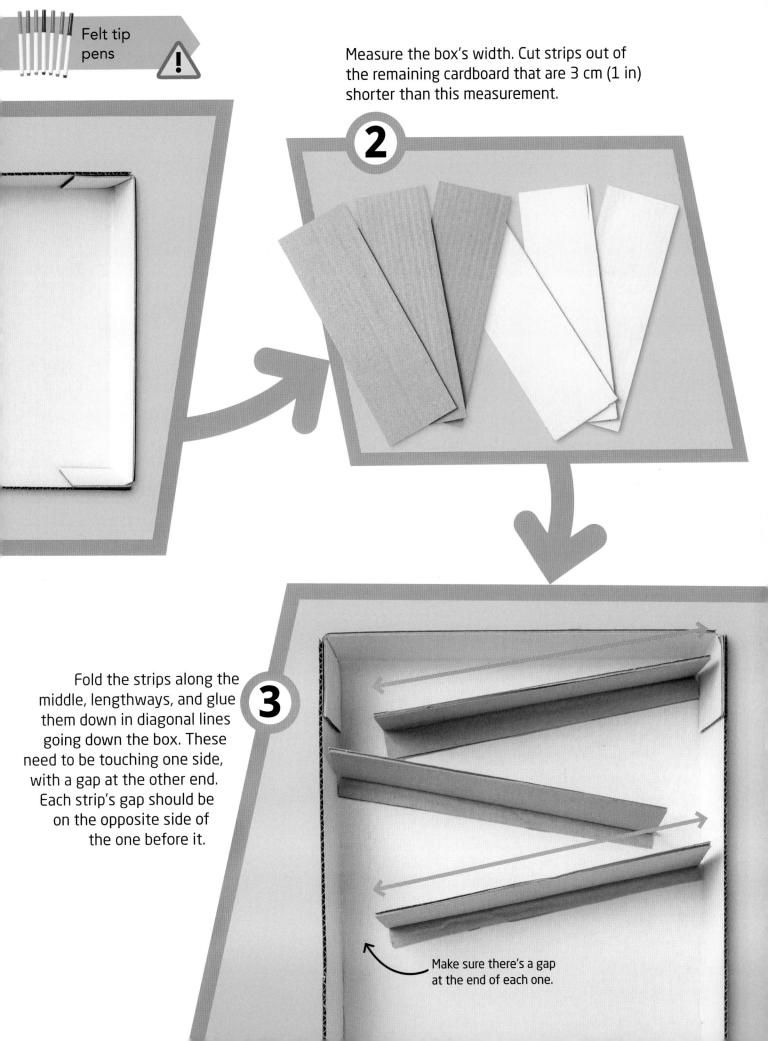

Measure the box's width. Cut strips out of the remaining cardboard that are 3 cm (1 in) shorter than this measurement.

2

Fold the strips along the middle, lengthways, and glue them down in diagonal lines going down the box. These need to be touching one side, with a gap at the other end. Each strip's gap should be on the opposite side of the one before it.

3

Make sure there's a gap at the end of each one.

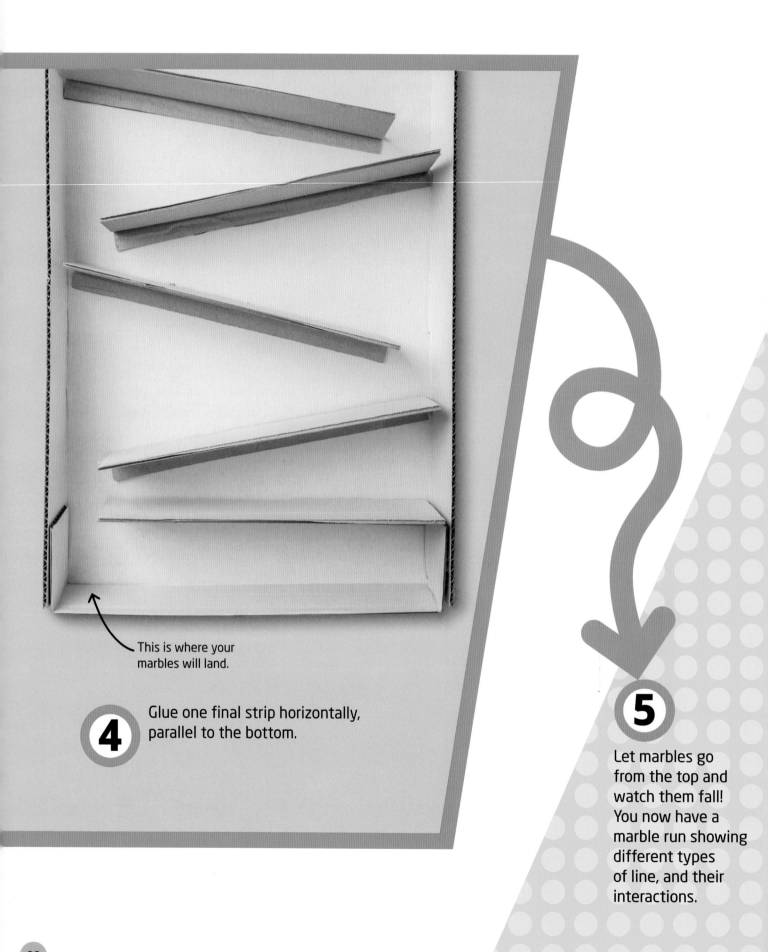

This is where your
marbles will land.

4 Glue one final strip horizontally,
parallel to the bottom.

5

Let marbles go
from the top and
watch them fall!
You now have a
marble run showing
different types
of line, and their
interactions.

Perpendicular line

Parallel line

Perpendicular line

Vertical line

Let the marbles go from the top.

Diagonal line

Parallel line

Decorate the marble run with different designs.

Horizontal line

93

Gladys
West

Mathematician • Born in 1930 • From the USA

Gladys West realised as a young girl that she didn't want to work on her parents' farm. Instead, she chose to study maths and science. Her calculations and discoveries help millions of us navigate the world each day using a digital map system called GPS (Global Positioning System).

Astronomical Gladys

Gladys studied lots of data collected by satellites, which are unpiloted spacecraft orbiting (circling) Earth. She also gathered information about planets and objects in space. One of Gladys's discoveries was the link between how the dwarf planet Pluto and the planet Neptune move.

Satellites can gather information about lots of things, including weather.

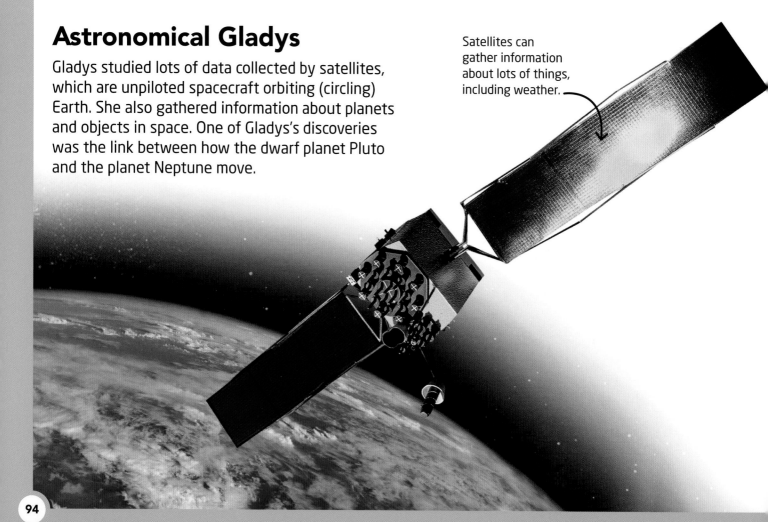

Pinpointing location

There are satellites in orbit above you now! Satellites send out signals, which tell computers on Earth – such as smartphones and tablets – how far away they are. Using this information, the computer can calculate its location exactly.

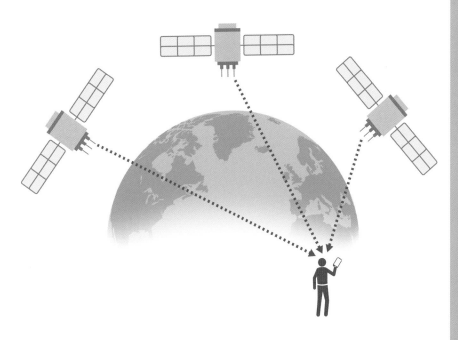

Computer wizardry

Gladys did lots of calculations by hand, as well as using early computers. She would programme room-sized 'supercomputers' to work out the location of oceans and other places on the Earth. All of this programming helped to develop GPS, which is used all over the world today.

Celebrating Gladys

Gladys wasn't rewarded for her important work for many years. However, her work was recently rediscovered. She's now in the United States Air Force Hall of Fame!

"When you're working every day, you're not thinking, 'What impact is this going to have on the world?' You're thinking, 'I've got to get this right.'"

Picture algorithm

You can use maths to describe pictures very precisely. This means you could help someone create a design without showing them a picture to copy. All you need is a set of precise instructions - an algorithm - to describe the picture.

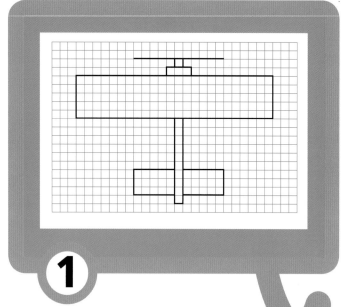

1

Draw a picture on the graph paper keeping to the outlines of the squares.

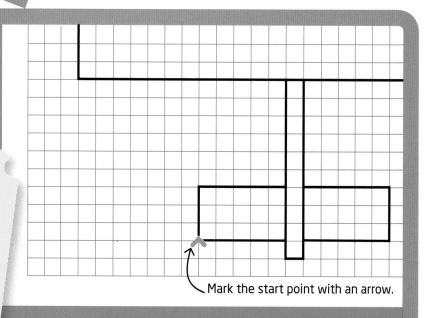

Mark the start point with an arrow.

* Start at the arrow.
* Draw a line forwards for three squares.
* Turn right.
* Draw a line forwards for five squares.
* Turn right.

2 Mark where to start with an arrow, to show which direction is forwards. Use the directions "right", "left", "forwards", and "backwards" to create instructions to make the same picture again.

Tell the drawer to move backwards when they get to the end of a line.

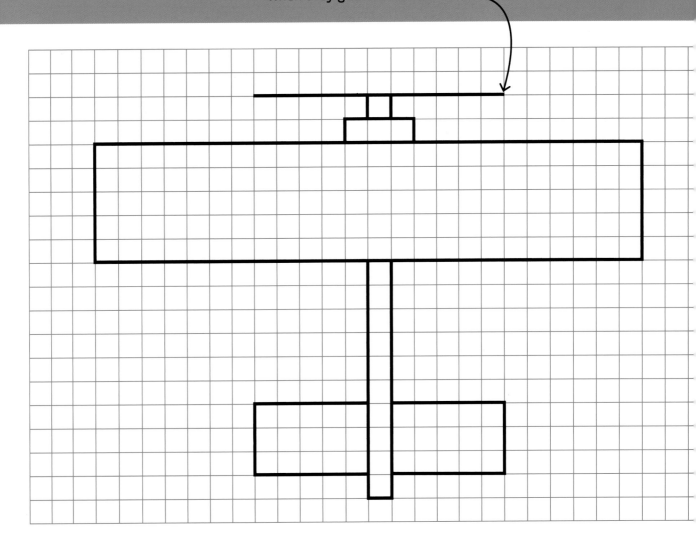

3 Give the instructions and blank graph paper to a friend. See if they can recreate the picture!

Now try...

For more advanced drawings, you could use angles to describe the turns. For example, to start a diagonal line, you could say "turn 45 degrees to the right, then move forwards...". Find out about angles on page 134.

Measure a circle

How do you measure the outside of a circle? A ruler on its own just won't do. You can find the distance around a small wheel by marking an arrow and taking it for a spin.

Circular measurements

When it comes to circles, there are three main measurements. The diameter is the distance from one side to the other. The radius is the distance from the middle to the outside, which is half the diameter. The circumference is around the outside.

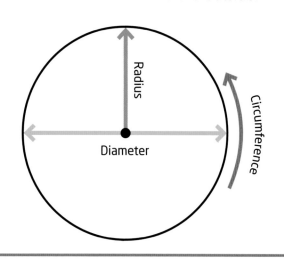

Radius

Diameter

Circumference

1 Create a wheel from card by drawing around the base of a bowl and cutting out the shape.

Carefully cut out the circle.

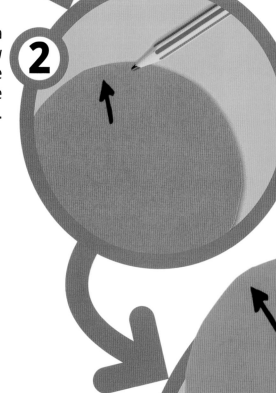

2 Draw a small arrow somewhere around the outside.

3 Place a ball of sticky tack beneath the centre of the wheel, on a hard surface. Carefully push a pencil through into the sticky tack. Keep the pencil in place.

Make sure you move the wheel in a straight line!

Mark the start point.

Place the wheel on paper with the arrow pointing down. Roll the wheel in a straight line until the arrow hits the paper again. The distance between these points is the circumference!

4

Use a ruler to measure the line when you've finished.

→ ## Now try...

To find the circumference of a circle with a calculator, measure the diameter with a ruler and multiply it by 3.14. This number is called pi (π).

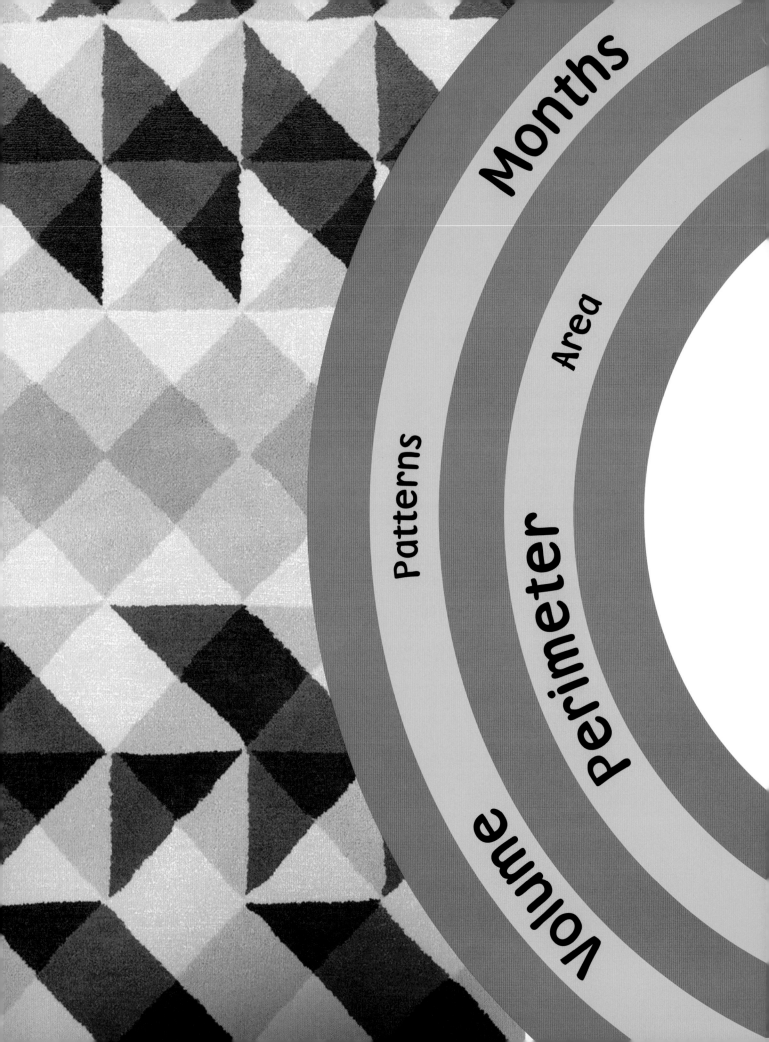

Months

Area

Patterns

Perimeter

Volume

Around the home

If you're reading this at home, how big is the room in which you're sitting? You'll need to use mathematical skills to measure it. There's probably maths elsewhere around you, too. Think about patterns, calendars, and growing plants.

Days

Calendars

Co-ordinates

Length

Data

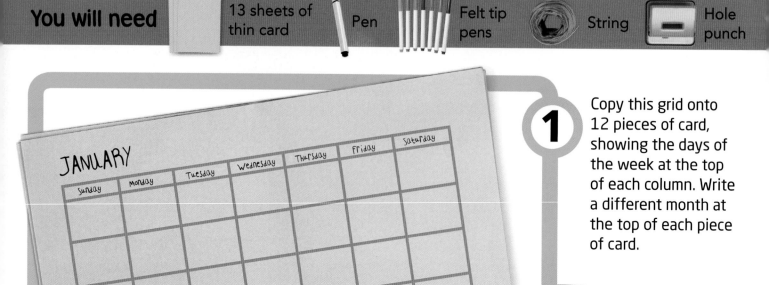

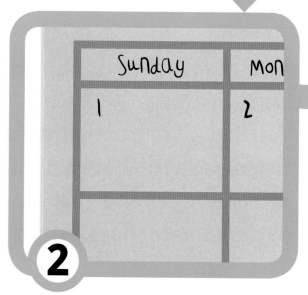

1 Copy this grid onto 12 pieces of card, showing the days of the week at the top of each column. Write a different month at the top of each piece of card.

Make a calendar

You can track time using a calendar. It shows the current day of the week, and the month of the year. It also helps you remember important dates, such as birthdays. Follow the steps on these pages to make your very own calendar!

2 Ask an adult to help you find a calendar on the internet, to learn the dates for each month of the coming year. Write each date into the correct box, in the column showing its day of the week.

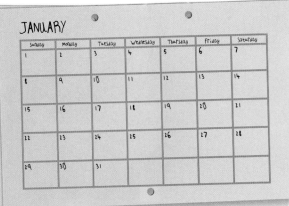

JANUARY

Sunday	Monday	Tuesday	Wednesday	Thursday	Friday	Saturday
1	2	3	4	5	6	7
8	9	10	11	12	13	14
15	16	17	18	19	20	21
22	23	24	25	26	27	28
29	30	31				

3 Place the 12 sheets of card on top of one another, with the grid facing up, and put a blank sheet on the top. Punch two holes in the top of all 13. Tie each set of holes up with string. Punch one hole in the centre at the bottom of all 13.

You could put string through the top holes to hang the calendar up. Untie this to change the month over.

Decorate the calendar with pictures.

You could match the string to the calendar's background colour.

4 Unfold each month and stick a photograph or a picture on to the blank card above it. Use the hole above each picture to hang the calendar from a hook or nail in the wall.

APRIL

Sunday	Monday	Tuesday	Wednesday	Thursday	Friday	Saturday
		1	2	3	4	5
6	7	8	9	10	11	12
13	14	15	16	17	18	19

1

Many household objects can be used as stamps. For example, you can cut sponge or paper into any shape you want. Find some objects to use as stamps.

Sponges

Kitchen roll

2

Carefully dip your stamps in fabric paint and try out different patterns on a piece of paper. Once you've decided which patterns you like, you're ready to print them on an old T-shirt.

Printing patterns

Mathematicians often look out for patterns, or when things are repeated in a sequence. Some patterns are made up of shapes. Try making your own patterns to put on a T-shirt!

Scissors   Iron   Plain T-Shirt

3 Press your stamps onto the T-shirt to make your patterns. Hold the stamps down firmly so there is a clear layer of paint on the fabric.

4 Once the ink has dried, ask an adult to iron it for you, without steam. This will make sure the paint stays on the T-shirt.

If you overlap shapes, be careful not to use too much ink or the patterns may not be clear to see.

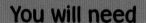
1 Measure all the walls in your room using measuring tape. Write down the measurements of each wall.

To learn more about measurements, turn to pages 22–23.

Draw the shape of your room on graph paper, using one square to show 1 m (roughly 3 ft) of wall. Round up or down if the wall is too short or long to fit neatly into the squares.

A 3 m (10 ft) wall would be three squares long.

2

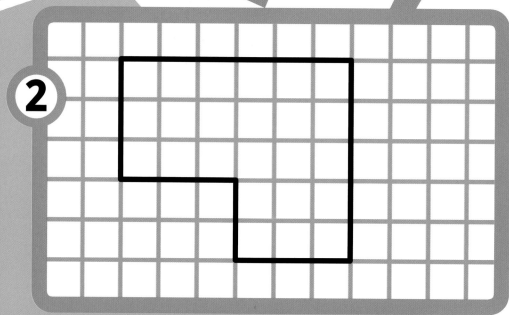

Create a floor plan

It's useful to know how much space there is in your room in case you want to rearrange your furniture. Your bed might not fit against your shortest wall! Floor plans show a room's area. Follow these steps to make a plan of your room.

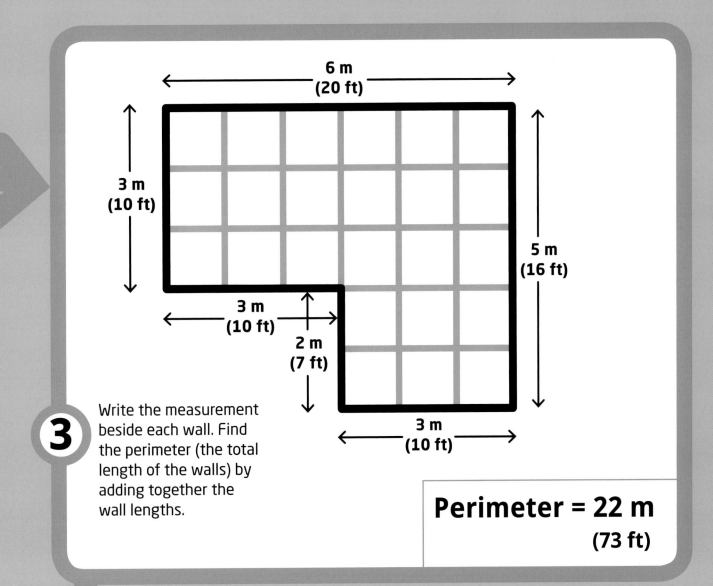

6 m
(20 ft)

3 m
(10 ft)

5 m
(16 ft)

3 m
(10 ft)

2 m
(7 ft)

3 m
(10 ft)

3 Write the measurement beside each wall. Find the perimeter (the total length of the walls) by adding together the wall lengths.

Perimeter = 22 m
(73 ft)

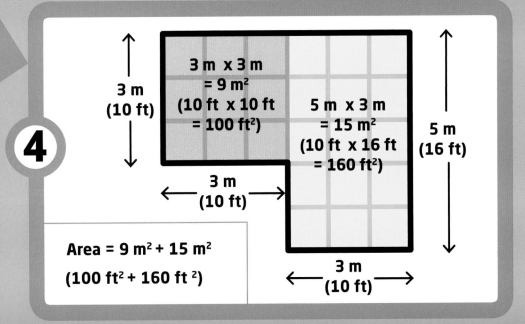

3 m
(10 ft)

3 m x 3 m
= 9 m²
(10 ft x 10 ft
= 100 ft²)

5 m x 3 m
= 15 m²
(10 ft x 16 ft
= 160 ft²)

5 m
(16 ft)

3 m
(10 ft)

3 m
(10 ft)

4 Find the area. If your room is a rectangle, such as a square, multiply the length by the width. If the room isn't rectangular, divide it into rectangles. Then find the area for each section, and add the answers together.

Area = 9 m² + 15 m²

(100 ft² + 160 ft ²)

Benjamin Banneker

Polymath • 1731-1806 • From the USA

Benjamin Banneker was a polymath, which means someone who knows about lots of subjects! He was excellent at learning things by himself, rather than at school. Through a love of reading, he taught himself about mathematics, astronomy (the study of natural objects in space), history, and even how to make clocks.

Timekeeper

Once, Benjamin saw a pocket watch and decided to create one himself, from scratch. As a young man, he carved cogs and wheels from wood, and put a much larger clock together. It was incredibly accurate and worked for the rest of his life. It was one of the first of its kind in America, but was sadly destroyed in a fire on the day of Benjamin's funeral.

Written in the stars

Benjamin became a keen astronomer after being shown a telescope, which is an instrument for looking at things a long way away. He learned astronomy, and wrote books filled with calculations and diagrams (drawings) showing the position of the stars. He used his findings to correctly predict a solar eclipse in 1789 - something which many astronomers didn't see coming.

A solar eclipse is when the Moon blocks out the Sun.

The lay of the land

Benjamin did important work as a surveyor, which is someone who measures land. He was asked to join the team working on a new American city called Washington D.C., which would be the country's capital! He used astronmy to provide information about the area, and help plan where things should go in the city.

This early map shows Washington D.C., USA.

"The colour of the skin is in no way connected with strength of the mind."

Maths for everyone

When Benjamin was alive, many people thought that black people weren't as smart as others. Benjamin proved them wrong by releasing books called almanacs about all the things he knew. He believed everyone was equal and tried to convince Thomas Jefferson, who would become the American president, to end slavery (the system that allowed people to own other people).

Benjamin wrote six almanacs.

Copy the graph below.
At the end of each week,
you'll add an "x" mark to show
the height of your sunflower.

1

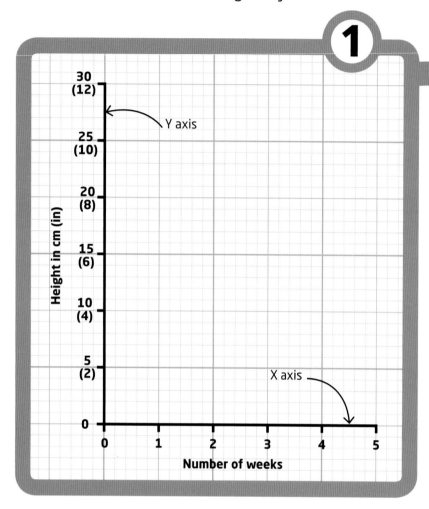

2

Follow the instructions
on a packet of sunflower
seeds to plant your seed.

Sunflower size

**Sunflowers can grow very tall - maybe even taller than
you! If you measure a sunflower regularly, you can keep
track of how tall it is, and work out how fast it is growing.
A scatter graph is an easy way to show this information.**

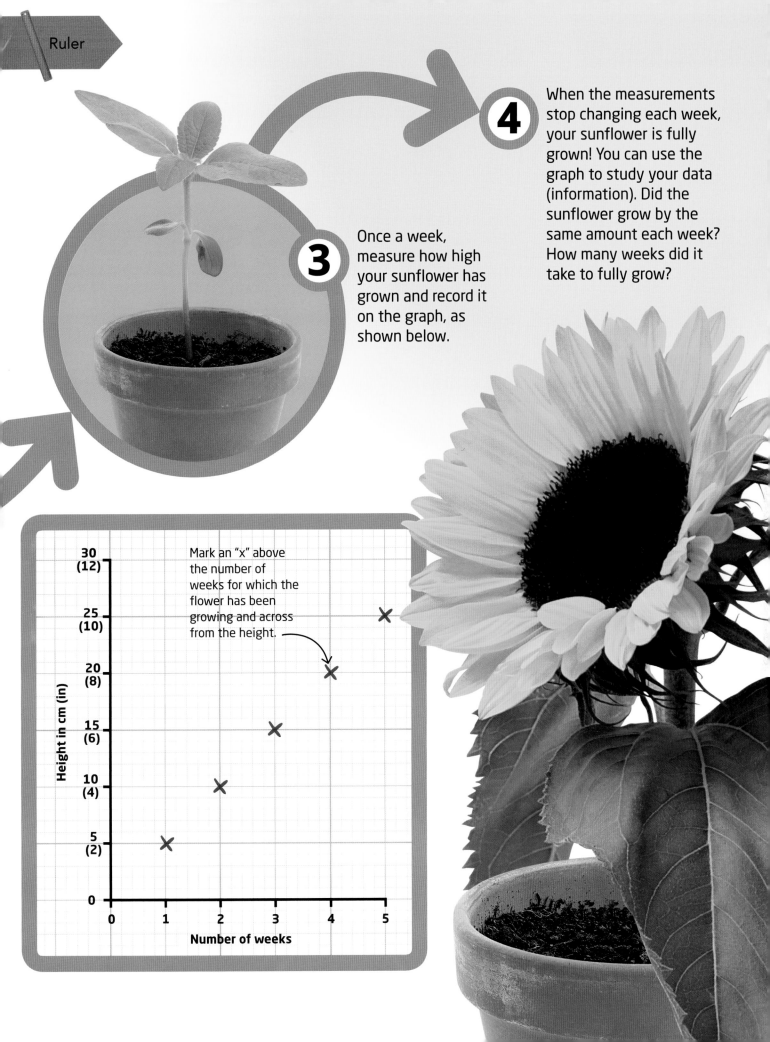

Ruler

Once a week, measure how high your sunflower has grown and record it on the graph, as shown below.

3

4 When the measurements stop changing each week, your sunflower is fully grown! You can use the graph to study your data (information). Did the sunflower grow by the same amount each week? How many weeks did it take to fully grow?

Mark an "x" above the number of weeks for which the flower has been growing and across from the height.

Height in cm (in)

30 (12)

25 (10)

20 (8)

15 (6)

10 (4)

5 (2)

0

0   1   2   3   4   5

Number of weeks

Ruler

Treasure-map co-ordinates

You can use mathematical skills to make a treasure map! Follow the steps on these pages to create a map, plan a treasure hunt, and use co-ordinates to mark where the clues and treasure are.

Pick a room with lots of places to hide things behind.

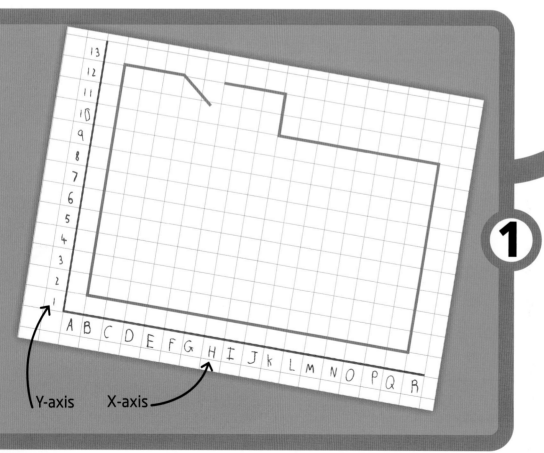

1 Draw x- and y-axes near the edges of your paper. Add letters to the x-axis, and numbers to the y-axis, starting at the bottom. Then, draw the outline of your room.

Y-axis   X-axis

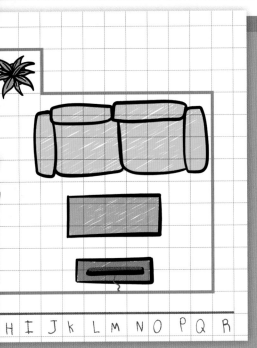

H I J K L M N O P Q R

Draw furniture and other things in the room on the map. Make sure these match up to where they are in real life.

2

Map co-ordinates

On a map, the x-axis and y-axis make it easy to plot a point. For the x co-ordinate, trace down with your finger until you hit a letter on the x-axis. For the y co-ordinate, trace along with your finger until you hit a number on the y-axis.

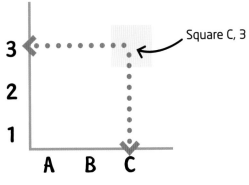

Square C, 3

Axes can show letters or numbers.

3

Choose hiding places for clues, then find their x and y co-ordinates on the map. Write each co-ordinate down on a scrap of paper, along with a clue number.

Clue 1
H, 11

Clue 2
M, 2

The x co-ordinate is the x-axis letter below the point.

Clue 3
0, 9

The y co-ordinate is the y-axis number it is level with.

Hide Clue 1 and mark an "x" on the map to show where it is. Hide Clue 2 at the co-ordinates in Clue 1. Hide Clue 3 at the co-ordinates in Clue 2, and so on.

4

Doors can be drawn like this on maps.

13
12
11
10
9
8
7
6
5
4
3
2
1

A B C D E F G H I J K L M N O P Q

Decide where you're going to hide the treasure and write these co-ordinates on the final clue.

5

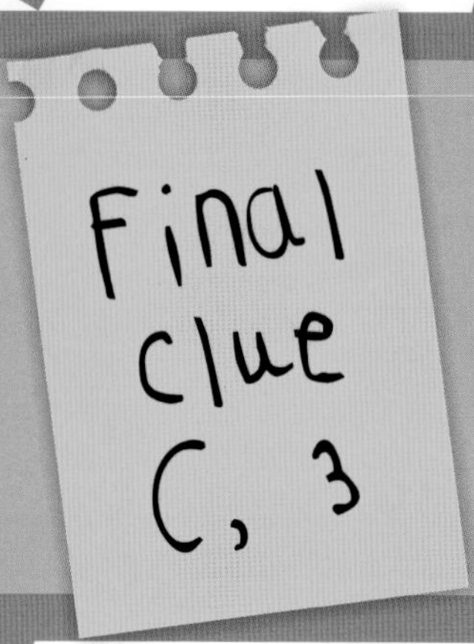

Final clue
C, 3

Wrap up your treasure in a box and hide it at the location in the final clue. Make sure it's well-hidden, or it might be found early!

6

TREASURE

13
12
11
10
9
8
7
6
5
4
3

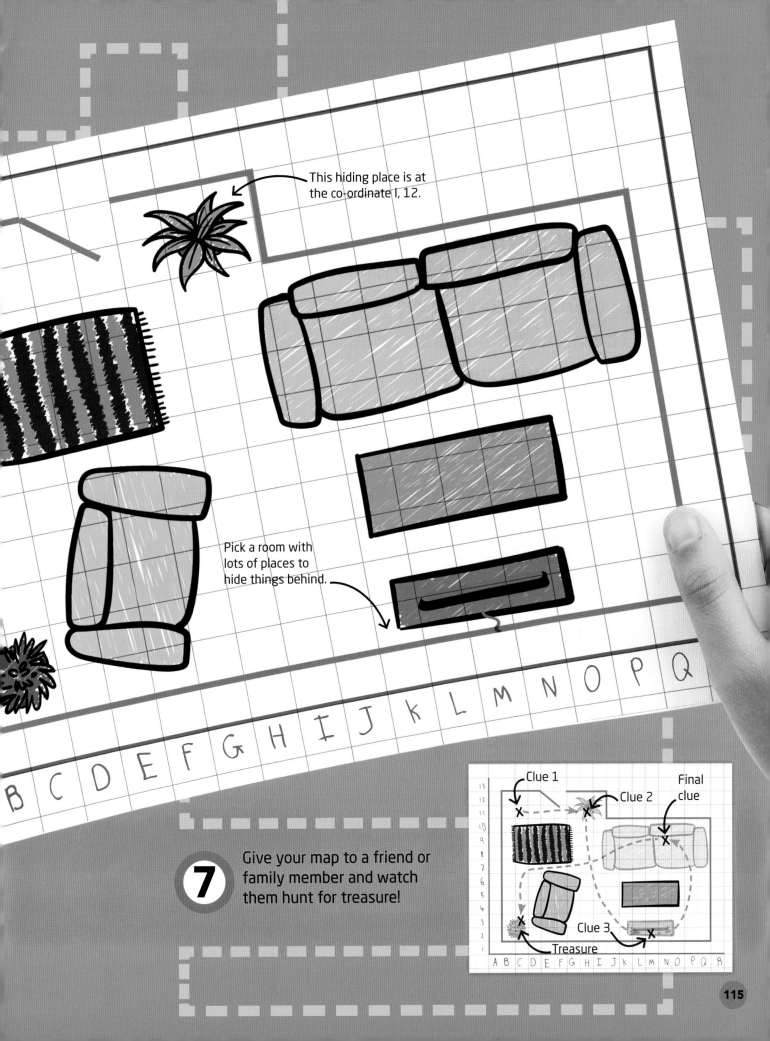

This hiding place is at the co-ordinate I, 12.

Pick a room with lots of places to hide things behind.

B C D E F G H I J K L M N O P Q

7 Give your map to a friend or family member and watch them hunt for treasure!

Clue 1   Clue 2   Final clue

13 12 11 10 9 8 7 6 5 4 3 2 1

Treasure   Clue 3

A B C D E F G H I J K L M N O P Q R

Computer maths

Computers follow instructions in order to do different things, such as showing words or colours on a screen. These instructions are called computer code. Just like humans, computers can follow instructions in different languages.

Coding languages

Languages for computers are called programming languages. These have their own rules, so the instructions are written in different ways.

Mathematical symbols such as ">" (greater than) might be part of code.

```
if (score >5) {
showWinnerScreen ()
}
else {
showGameOverScreen ()
```

This is an example of the computer language Java.

Some instructions are written as they might be for a human, but without spaces.

Algorithms

A set of instructions is called an algorithm. Like a recipe, it tells the computer how to complete a task. Can you write an algorithm for making a pizza?

1. Add tomato sauce to the base.

2. Add grated cheese to the base.

3. Bake the pizza.

4. Add basil to the cooked pizza.

True or false?

Computers check whether a statement in their code is either true or false. If it is true, then the computer does one thing. If false, then it does something different. Let's look at how the coding might work for the end screen of a game. In the game, you play as a unicorn and must collect 10 rainbows in under 30 seconds to win.

Score 9

The code tells the computer to show a winner screen if your score hits 10.

If time runs out and you haven't scored 10, the code tells the computer to show a "Game Over" screen.

Winner

Game Over

Calculations, calculations

A computer is an amazing maths tool. They are able to do millions of calculations in a second. The fastest supercomputers in the world can do many billions of calculations in a second!

Supercomputers are much bigger than the computers in homes and schools.

Tomohiro Nishikado

Video-game developer • Born in 1944 • From Japan

In video games, computer code makes characters move, adds up scores, allows you to control what is happening in the game, and much, much more! Tomohiro 'Tom-Tom' Nishikado invented the code for one of the most popular video games of all time – *Space Invaders*.

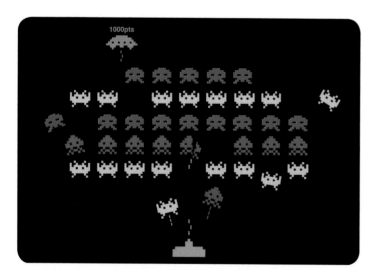

1000pts

"I had no idea the game would become so popular."

Space Invaders

After working on lots of different video games, Tomohiro started designing *Space Invaders* in 1977. The player controlled a spaceship that battled aliens, which were attacking it. Tomohiro designed the characters, sounds, and score system.

Space Invaders started out as an arcade game, which means it was housed in its own special machine.

Gaming maths

Making a video game is much easier if you're a maths whizz. As well as writing computer code for the game, you might need to design a scoring system, which uses maths to add up points. Designers also have to think about how long the game will run, how fast the graphics (images) will move, and the sizes of characters on screen.

Games, games, games

Tomohiro said he prefers making games to playing them. Although *Space Invaders* is his most popular game, he's still working in the industry and has made games such as *Soccer*, a football game, and the car-racing game, *Speed Race*.

Top score

In early video games, the score was only shown once, at the end of each game, and then forgotten. Tomohiro changed this with *Space Invaders*. Scores from every game were stored, and the highest one became the 'top score' for other players to beat.

5
4
3
2
1

Body clock

Weight

Shoe size

Reflex

Acute

Height

Obtuse

Graphs

Correlation

Your body

When you weigh yourself or measure your height, you're using maths skills. Your body is also a helpful tool to help you understand mathematical topics – you can count using your fingers and make angles with your arms!

Data collection

1 Cut out a circle from card. Using a protractor, mark a line every 30° around the top half. Use the straight edge of the protractor to draw a line in pencil across the circle from each mark.

Draw pen lines a short way into either end of each line, then rub out the pencil. Turn over the circle and repeat steps one and two.

2

Make your body clock

Your body has an internal clock that changes how you feel throughout the day. For example, you probably feel hungry in the mornings and sleepy at night. Now try making a clock out of card, to show how your body clock affects you.

Colouring pencils

Scissors

Hole punch

Ribbon

3 Write the numbers 1-12 beneath the lines on each side, just like they appear on a clock. On one side, write "a.m." in the middle; on the other, write "p.m.".

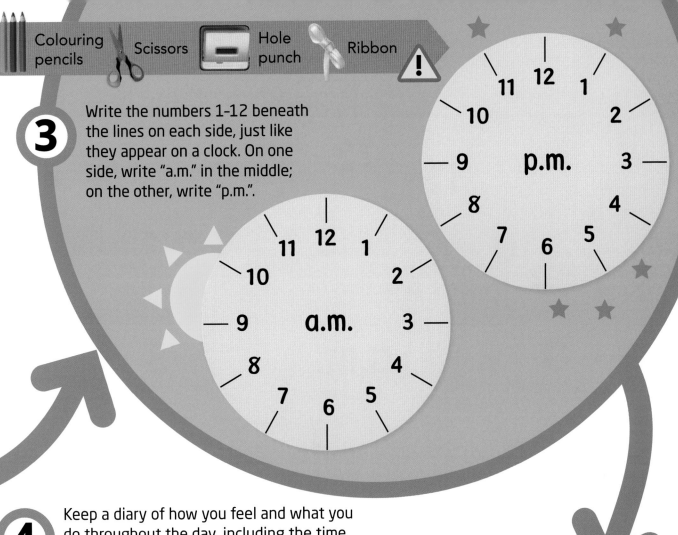

p.m.

a.m.

4 Keep a diary of how you feel and what you do throughout the day, including the time you wake up, when you feel hungry, when you've got lots of energy, when you feel tired, and when you go to sleep!

6 a.m.– 9 a.m.
Woke up, feeling much less sleepy than when I went to bed. Hungry for breakfast.

9 a.m.– 12 p.m.
Concentrated lots on work at school. Remembered lots of facts.

12 p.m.– 1 p.m.
Felt hungry, had lunch.

1 p.m.– 3 p.m.
Felt sleepy after a big meal at lunch. Was less good at P.E. than normal!

● 3 p.m.– 5 p.m.
Ran about, was faster than at break time. Didn't feel as tired as earlier.

5 p.m.– 6 p.m.
Felt hungry! Dinner time.

● 6 p.m.– 7 p.m.
Felt sleepy again.

7 p.m.–6 a.m. I was asleep!

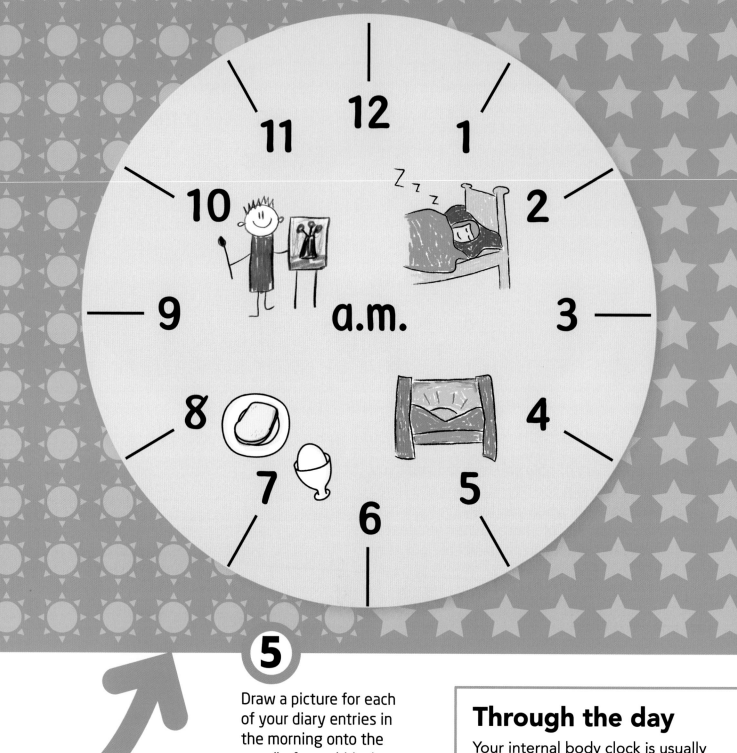

5

Draw a picture for each of your diary entries in the morning onto the a.m. (before midday) side of your clock. Then add pictures to the p.m. side too.

Through the day

Your internal body clock is usually matched to the Sun's light, which changes throughout the day. It helps you follow a routine, so you feel sleepy at night, and full of energy in the day. After the 24 hours of the day are up, the clock begins its work again!

p.m.

Make a hole using a hole punch and thread ribbon through. Hang the clock up to show the a.m. side in the morning and turn it over at midday.

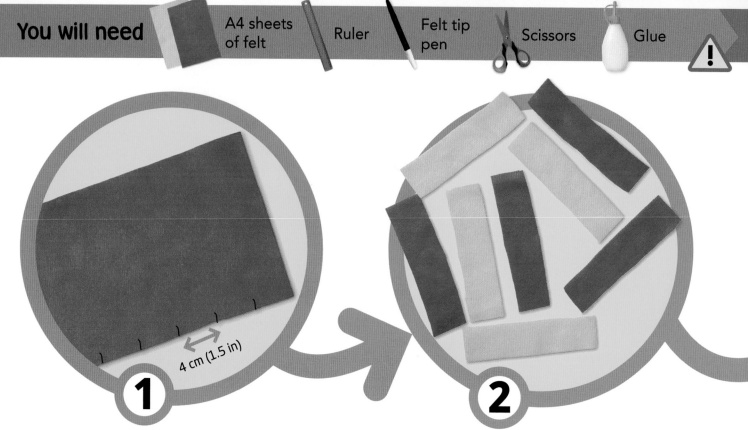

1 Fold the felt in half lengthways and mark 11 lines along the edge opposite to the fold, about every 4 cm (1.5 in).

4 cm (1.5 in)

2 Carefully cut in a straight line from each mark to divide the felt into 11 strips.

Finger place value

Every digit in a number has a different place value. Let's make finger puppets for the digits zero to nine and a decimal point. You can use these to form different numbers and become a whizz at recognising place value.

This puppet currently has a place value of ten thousand.

Turn to pages 13 and 88 — to learn about place value and decimal numbers

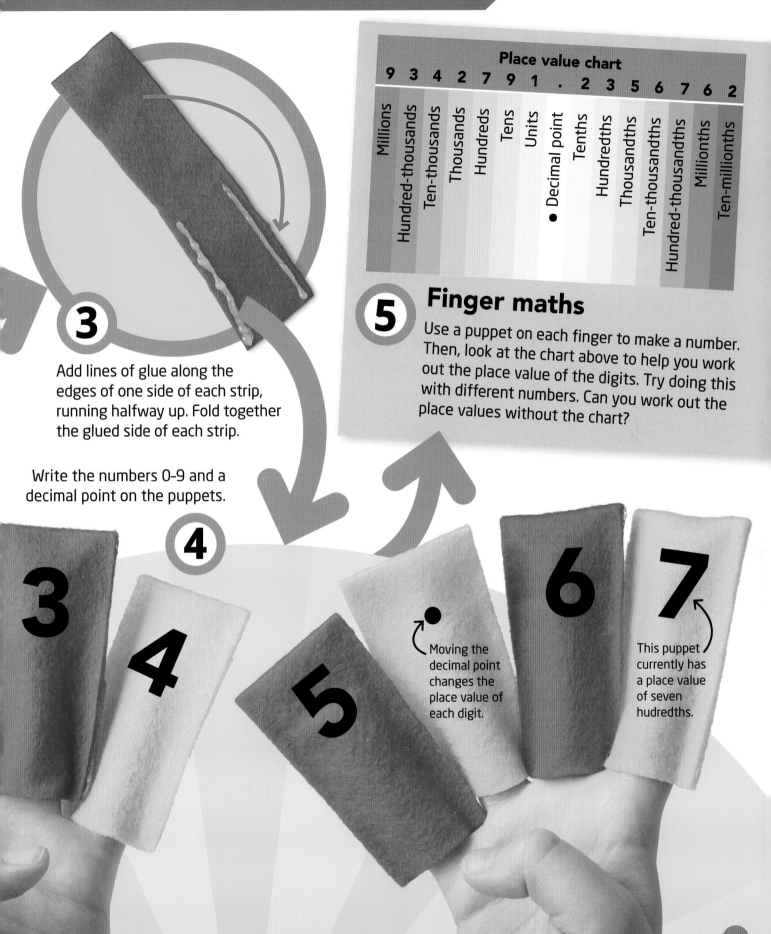

Place value chart

9	3	4	2	7	9	1	.	2	3	5	6	7	6	2
Millions	Hundred-thousands	Ten-thousands	Thousands	Hundreds	Tens	Units	Decimal point	Tenths	Hundredths	Thousandths	Ten-thousandths	Hundred-thousandths	Millionths	Ten-millionths

3

Add lines of glue along the edges of one side of each strip, running halfway up. Fold together the glued side of each strip.

Write the numbers 0–9 and a decimal point on the puppets.

4

5 Finger maths

Use a puppet on each finger to make a number. Then, look at the chart above to help you work out the place value of the digits. Try doing this with different numbers. Can you work out the place values without the chart?

3 4 5 6 7

Moving the decimal point changes the place value of each digit.

This puppet currently has a place value of seven hudredths.

What are statistics?

Gathering information, or data, helps us understand things better. Data can be converted into numbers, known as statistics, which can be displayed in different ways. Here are some statistics on popular pets...

Venn diagram

A clear way to sort data is using a Venn diagram. Each circle represents a category, or group that the animals can be sorted into, with the overlap showing where they fit into more than one category.

FURRY PETS

An animal that fits into all three categories goes into the centre segment.

Tally chart

Tally charts are a great way to collect data quickly and easily. First, choose a question to ask your friends, then record each answer given with a vertical mark against that option. For every fifth tally mark, you strike through the other four diagonally.

What's your favourite pet?

FAVOURITE	TALLY	NUMBER
Dog	̸|||| ̸||||	10
Tortoise	|||	3
Fish	||||	4
Cat	̸||||	5
Pony			1
Parrot	|||	3

Sets of five can be counted easily.

Count up the tally marks to find the total.

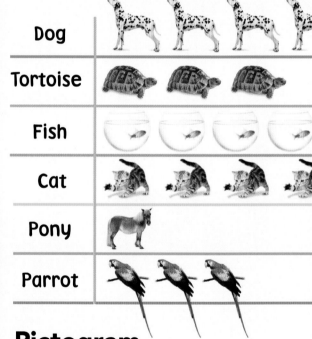

Dog	
Tortoise	
Fish	
Cat	
Pony	
Parrot	

Pictogram

Pictures can be used to represent data. In a pictogram, they are divided into rows or columns, so they're easy to count up.

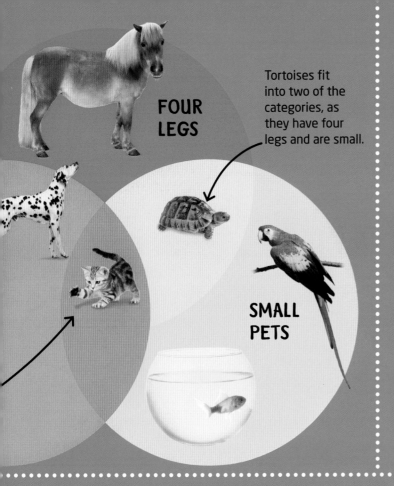

FOUR LEGS

Tortoises fit into two of the categories, as they have four legs and are small.

SMALL PETS

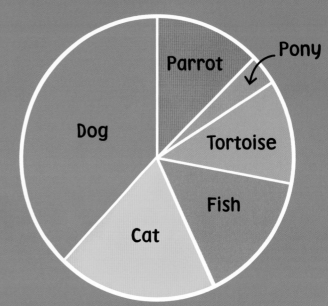

Parrot

Pony

Dog

Tortoise

Fish

Cat

Pie chart

Pie charts are handy for showing how popular different options are in comparison to each other. Dogs have the biggest slice, so are the most popular. Ponies, with the smallest portion of the pie, are the least popular.

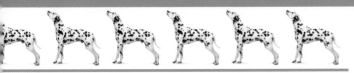

Axis

| 0 | 2 | 4 | 6 | 8 | 10 |

Dog

Tortoise

Fish

Cat

Pony

Parrot

Bar chart
You can easily turn the pictures in a pictogram into a bar to make a bar chart. The height or length of the bar lines up with a number on the axis.

Voting

Statistics can be very important. Whether it's a vote on an award at school or for a political party to govern a country, statistics help us organise data.

Each vote is counted, with the person, or people, who receive the biggest vote named the winners.

129

Data discovery

Data is another word for pieces of information. You can use maths to describe facts about data, to create summaries called statistics. For example, the average (normal) shoe size for a group of friends is a statistic. Now it's time to find your own statistics!

1 Ask seven of your friends to tell you their age, height, and shoe size.

I'm 7 years old.

I'm 8 years old.

105 cm (41 in)

119 cm (47 in)

1

2

2 Find the mean

The mean is a type of average. Calculate the mean height of your friends by adding up all of the heights, and dividing the total by the number of friends. It might help to use a calculator.

$$105 + 119 + 142 + 125 + 115 + 129 + 112 = 847$$

$$847 \div 7 = 121$$

Number of friends

Mean height in cm

Total height in cm

3 Find the median

The median is another type of average. Calculate the median age of your friends by writing down all of the ages in order from youngest to oldest, and then selecting the one in the very middle of the list.

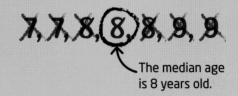

7, 7, 8, 8, 8, 9, 9

The median age is 8 years old.

4 Find the mode

The mode tells you the most common shoe size – it's another type of average! You can use a tally chart like the one below to work it out.

Shoe size	Tally	Number of friends
1	II	2
(2) ← The mode	III	3
2.5	II	2

The shoe size alongside the biggest number of friends is the mode.

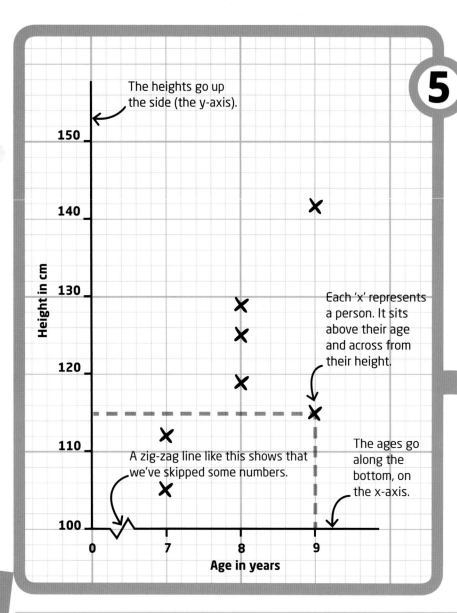

The heights go up the side (the y-axis).

Each 'x' represents a person. It sits above their age and across from their height.

A zig-zag line like this shows that we've skipped some numbers.

The ages go along the bottom, on the x-axis.

Height in cm

150
140
130
120
110
100

0   7   8   9

Age in years

5

To find out how age affects height, draw a scatter graph like the one here. Write the ages along the bottom, and height up the side. To plot a friend's height, trace up from their age and across from their height until your fingers meet.

What is correlation?

Correlation is the relationship between data. A **positive correlation** means that as one data set increases, so does the other. A **negative correlation** means that as one data set increases, the other decreases. No correlation means that two data sets aren't related.

In hot weather people eat more ice cream. This is a positive correlation.

In snowy weather people eat less ice cream. This is a negative correlation.

 ?

Owning a dog doesn't make a difference to how much ice cream people eat! This is no correlation.

6 Use a coloured pencil to draw a line roughly through the middle of the points.

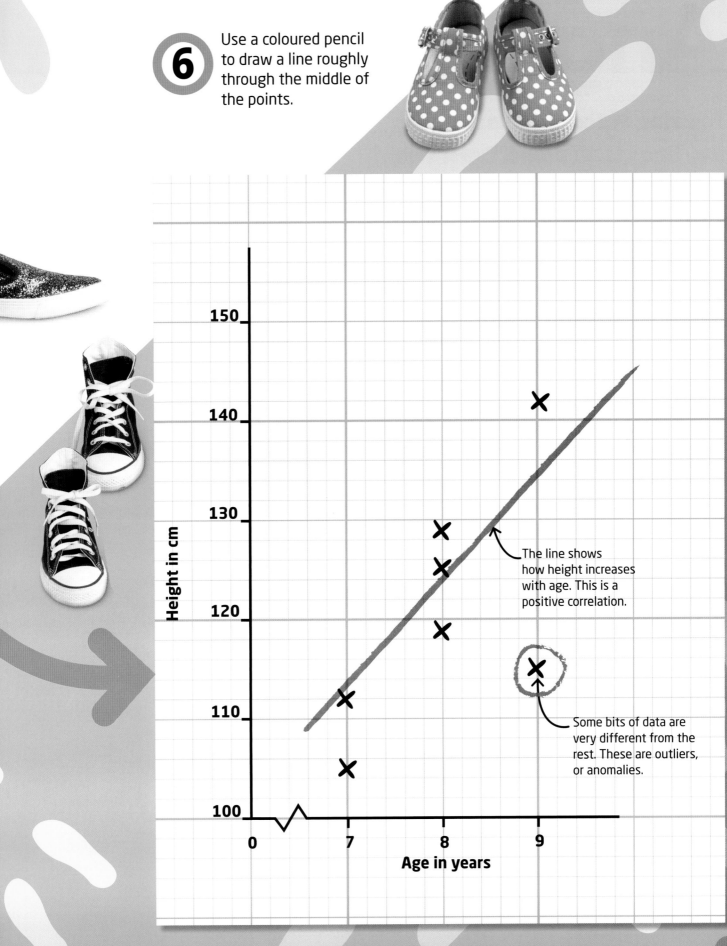

The line shows how height increases with age. This is a positive correlation.

Some bits of data are very different from the rest. These are outliers, or anomalies.

Height in cm

Age in years

Angles

The size of the turn between two lines is an angle. Draw two straight lines that are touching each other at one end. You've just created two angles! There's an angle between the lines and a larger angle around the outside.

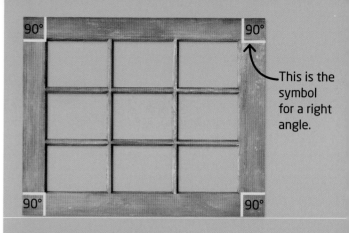

This is the symbol for a right angle.

Right angles

A right angle measures exactly 90°. The four angles in the corners of any rectangle are right angles. You can spot right angles on lots of things - windows, doors, walls, books, and boxes are just a few examples!

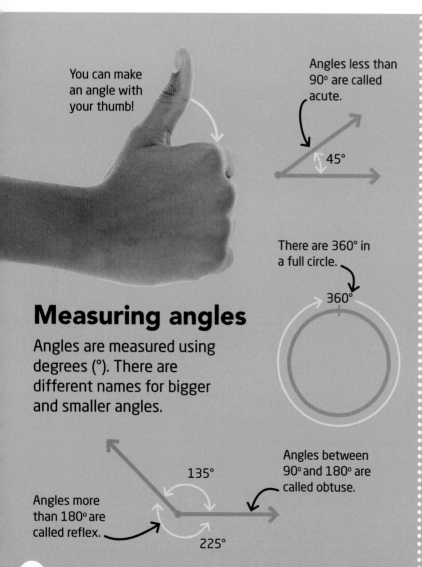

You can make an angle with your thumb!

Angles less than 90° are called acute.

45°

There are 360° in a full circle.

360°

Measuring angles

Angles are measured using degrees (°). There are different names for bigger and smaller angles.

Angles more than 180° are called reflex.

135°

Angles between 90° and 180° are called obtuse.

225°

Triangles

The name "triangle" means "three angles" ("tri" means "three" in Latin and Greek). This helps us remember that there are three angles in a triangle. If we add up all the degrees for these, the total is 180°. Try it - draw lots of triangles, use a protractor to measure the angles, and add them up. You'll always get 180°. Maths magic!

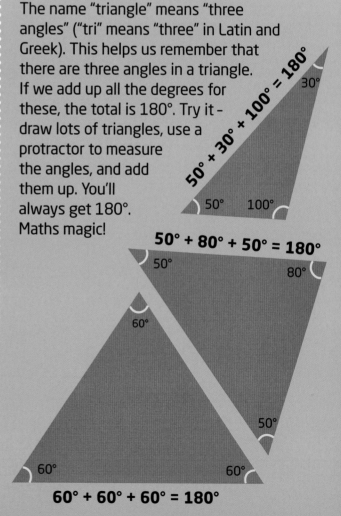

$50° + 30° + 100° = 180°$

30°

50°   100°

$50° + 80° + 50° = 180°$

50°

80°

60°

50°

$60° + 60° + 60° = 180°$

60°   60°

Arm angles

Lift your arms as high as you can.
How many angles can you make
with them? Start with your hands
touching above your head - that's 0°.
Then slowly lower them until they
are level - you are now at 180°. Can
you make a right angle? How about
an acute one? Just try not to
knock anything over!

Making turns

We use angles to describe the
size of turns. If you turn to face
in the opposite direction, that's
180° degrees. If you do a complete
spin, you have turned 360°.

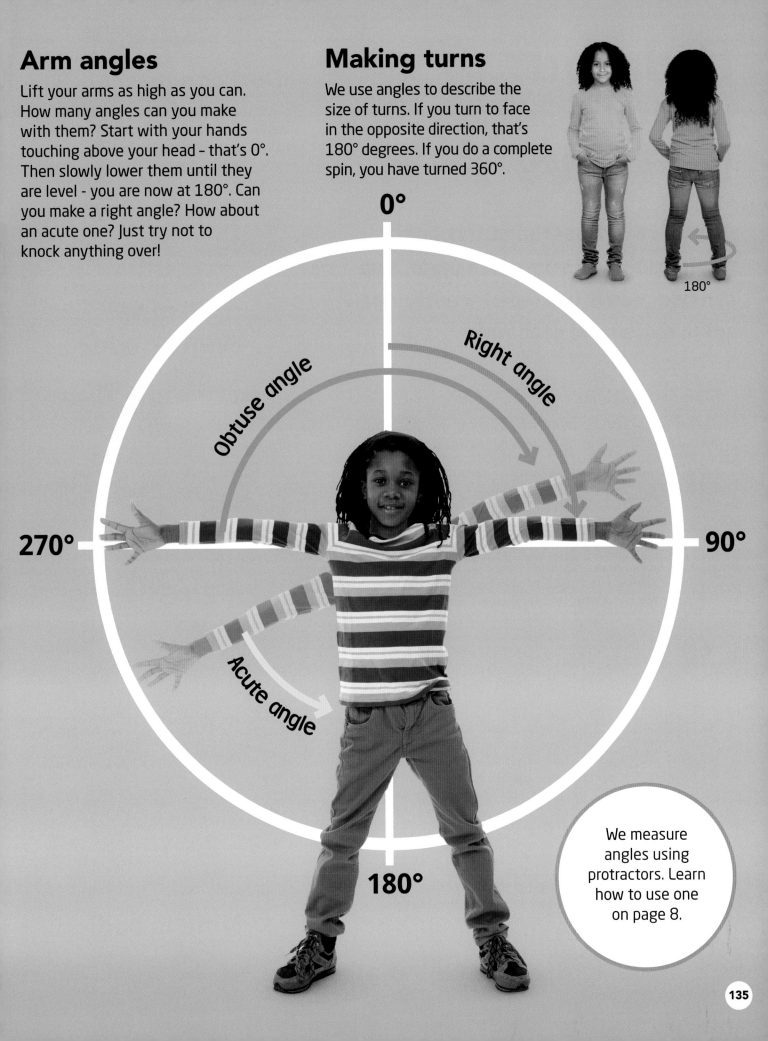

180°

0°

Obtuse angle

Right angle

270°

90°

Acute angle

180°

We measure
angles using
protractors. Learn
how to use one
on page 8.

Did you know?

As you've discovered in this book, maths isn't just sums on a page. You can use maths to predict weather or solve real-world problems.

Maths jobs

There are lots of different jobs you can do that involve working with numbers. Here are just a few.

Astronauts use lots of calculations to pilot spacecraft. To get into space they need to know the exact direction in which to travel and what their speed should be to safely leave the Earth's atmosphere.

Health analysts examine data about people's health so that hospitals and other medical institutions can be better run. They might look at how many people need a certain medicine so the right amount is ordered in the future.

Meteorologists measure the temperature, wind speed, and other data about the weather from all over the world. They use this information to help predict whether there'll be lots of sunshine or if a storm is coming!

Investment Managers help people invest their money. This means using money to make more money, for example by buying shares (parts of companies) and selling them for more than they cost.

Decision maths

Decision maths solves a problem. One example is an algorithm to work out whether you could divide a group into equal pairs. The group needs to be an even number to do this. If you kept removing two, you would be left with either one or zero – one means the number is odd, and zero means it's even!

Is nine even or odd?

9 – 2 = 7

Removing two hamsters from nine leaves seven.

7 – 2 = 5

Removing two hamsters from seven leaves five.

5 – 2 = 3

Removing two hamsters from five leaves three.

3 – 2 = 1

Removing two hamsters from three leaves one.

Nine is odd!

Computer numbers

Numbers form instructions in computer code. However, computers use different number systems to humans. For example, the hexadecimal system uses 16 symbols instead of just the nine Arabic digits. Hexadecimals are made up of the numbers 0–9 and the letters A–F.

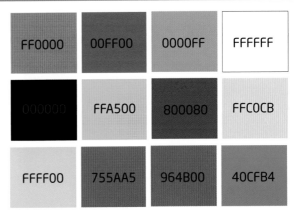

FF0000	00FF00	0000FF	FFFFFF
000000	FFA500	800080	FFC0CB
FFFF00	755AA5	964B00	40CFB4

Hexadecimals can be used in code to show colours on-screen. Every colour has a different number.

Number systems

The numbers we use in this book are Arabic numerals. Lots of other number systems have been used throughout history, and across the world.

Babylonian numerals
Around 4,000 years ago the Babylonian people (who lived in an area which is now part of Iraq and Syria) counted up grain and worked out other amounts using a system of numbers called cuneiform numerals.

1
2
3
4
5

Roman numerals
The Ancient Romans began using Latin letters to show different amounts more than 2,000 years ago. This system of numerals was used in Europe for many centuries after the fall of the Roman Empire, in 476 CE. It is still used on some clock faces and buildings in Europe today.

I — 1
II — 2
III — 3
IV — 4
V — 5

Hebrew alphabetic numerals
The most commonly used number system in Israel is Arabic. However, numbers which use letters from Hebrew, the Jewish language, are sometimes used for the Hebrew calendar and when numbering a list. These numbers emerged more than 2,200 years ago.

1
2
3
4
5

Chinese numerals
In China, money and certain other amounts are sometimes written down using Chinese characters. These can be written in different ways by different groups of people, such as people who work for banks.

一 — 1
二 — 2
三 — 3
四 — 4
五 — 5

Glossary

abacus Device used for counting or doing calculations, using beads to show different amounts

algorithm List of steps that tells you how to do something

a.m. Before midday (noon)

angle Size of turn between two lines that meet at a vertex (corner)

architecture Art of designing buildings

area Size of the space inside a shape

array Arrangement of objects or numbers into columns and rows

asymmetry When two halves of a shape or object don't perfectly match one another

average Normal amount in a set of data, such as the height that occurs most often in a group of children

bar chart Chart that uses rectangles to show amounts

calculation Something worked out mathematically

calculator Electronic device for doing sums

calendar Tables used to show the days, weeks, and months of a year

cipher Secret code for sending messages

circumference Distance around the outside of a circle

column addition Strategy for adding together large numbers

computer code Instructions telling a computer what to do

co-ordinate Number or letter from the axes of a graph (or map) used to describe a specific location

correlation Relationship between a set of data

cubed measurement Measurement of volume, calculated by multiplying together the length, width, and height

currency Coins and notes used in a particular place

data Information, such as numbers

decimal number Part of a whole number, which comes after a decimal point

decimal point Point that comes after whole numbers and before decimal numbers

degree Measurement of an angle

denominator Bottom number in a fraction

diagonal line Line running upwards or downwards on a slant

diameter Distance through the centre of a circle from one side to the other

digit Number from 0-9

distance Measurement of length from one point to another

division Splitting up a number or object into equal smaller amounts

double Multiply an amount by two

edge Line around the outside of a shape

face Surface of a 3D shape

fraction Part of a whole number or object

half The amount you're left with when you divide an amount into two equal parts

horizontal line Flat line

imperial unit Measurement from the imperial system of measurements, such as an inch (in)

mean Average found by adding together all the numbers in a set of data and dividing the answer by the total amount of numbers in the set

median The middle number in a set of data, when the data is arranged in order

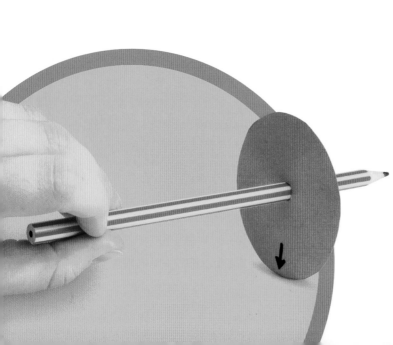

metric unit Measurement from the metric system of measurements, such as a centimetre (cm)

mode The number that occurs most often in a set of data

multiple Number that results from multiplying two numbers together

net Flat shape that can be folded to make a particular 3D shape

number bond Pair of numbers that can be added to make another number

number line Arrangement of numbers into a line that can be used for adding or subtracting

numerator Top number in a fraction

rotational symmetry When a shape can be rotated but still look the same

pattern Repeating sequence of numbers or shapes

perimeter Measurement around the outside of a shape

pictogram Graph that uses pictures to show information

pie chart Circular graph showing data as segments

place value Amount shown by a digit in a number

p.m. Time between midday and midnight

probability Likelihood of something happening

protractor Tool used to measure and draw angles

radius Distance from the centre of a circle to the outside

rectangle Shape with four straight sides and four right angles

right angle 90° angle

row Arrangement of numbers or items into a line

scatter graph Graph that uses marks arranged between horizontal and vertical axes to show data

sequence Set of numbers or things in a particular order

speed How fast something is going

squared measurement Measurement of area equal to the length multiplied by the height

statistic Piece of data

symmetry When two halves of a shape perfectly match each other

tally chart Chart that uses marks to show amounts

tessellation When shapes fit together without gaps

times table Table showing the multiples of a number

unit of measurement Standard size of a measurement, such as centimetres or inches

Venn diagram Diagram showing data grouped together in circles

vertex Point where two lines meet to form a corner, for example in a shape or angle

vertical line Line running straight up or down

volume Measurement of liquid or space inside a container

whole number Number with no fractions or decimals

x-axis Horizontal line used to measure position of marks on a graph

y-axis Vertical line used to measure position of marks on a graph

Index

12-hour clocks 82
24-hour clocks 82
2D shapes 26
3D shapes 26, 27, 28-29, 60-65

Aa
abaci 14-15
acute angles 134, 135
adding 15, 40, 43, 46-47, 107
age 130, 132-133
algorithms 96-97, 116
almanacs 109
a.m. 81, 82, 123, 124, 125
amounts 15, 21, 24-25, 40, 43, 44, 52, 57
angles 57, 97, 134-135

anomalies 133
arcade games 118
arches 56
architecture 56-59
area 22, 49, 106-107
array multiplication 74
arrays 74-75
astronomy 108, 109
asymmetrical objects 71
averages 130
axes 110-115, 129

Bb
banknotes 44, 45
Banneker, Benjamin 108-109
bar charts 129
birthdays 83, 102

Bletchley Park 36, 37
body clock 122-125
buildings 56-65

Cc
calculators 9, 99, 107
calendars 83, 102-103
car racing 86-87
categories 128
Celsius 23
change, money 46
churches 56-57
cipher wheel 38-39
ciphers 37, 38
circles 26, 98-99, 134
circular measurements 98-99
circumference 98
Clarke, Joan 36-37
clocks 80-83, 108
clues 113, 114
co-ordinates 112-115
code, computer 116-119
codebreaking 36-37
coins 44, 45
column addition 46-47
columns 74-75, 128
computers 95, 116-117
cone net 61, 65
cones 27, 56
corners 26, 27
correlation 132-133
counting 12-13, 15
cube net 62-63
cubed measurements 69
cubes 27, 28
cuboid nets 62-63, 64-65
cuboids 27, 68, 69
currency 44-47, 89
curves 58
cylinder net 62
cylinders 27

Dd
data 128-133
dates 83, 102

days 81, 82-83, 102, 125
decimal point 88, 126, 127
decimals 88-89
degrees 134
depth 69
designs 96-97, 119
diagonal lines 90, 91, 93, 97
diagrams 109
diameter 98
diaries 123, 124
die 19
digital clocks 82
digital maps 94-95
directions 94-95
distance, measuring 86-87
division 24, 50-53
dodecahedron net 64
doubling 24, 25

Ee
Earth 83, 95
edges 27, 28
eighths 17
energy 123, 125
engineering 57
Enigma code 37
equal amounts 52
equals sign 40, 41
equivalent fractions 17

Ff
faces 27, 28
Fahrenheit 23
falling bodies 84-85
false statements 117
finger puppets 126-127
floor plans 106-107
flowers, times table 76-77
foundations 57
fractions 13, 16-17, 89
fruit smoothie 24-25
furniture 59

Gg
general elections 129
geometry 27
GPS (Global Positioning System) 94-95
graph paper 96-97, 106-107, 110-111, 132-133
graphics 119

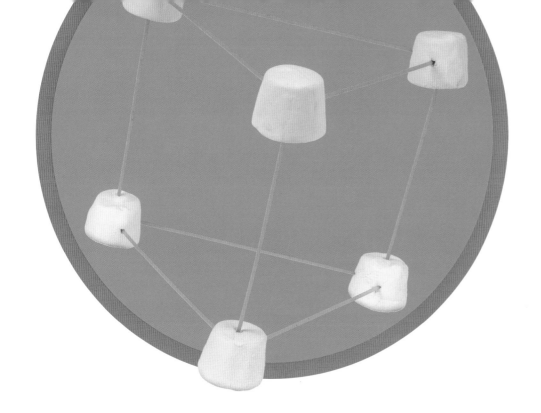

growth 110-111

Hh

Hadid, Zaha 58-59
Hagia Sophia (Turkey) 57
halves 17
halving 24, 25
height 22, 110-111, 69,
    129, 130-133
helicopters, timing 84-85
hexagonal pyramid net
    61, 62
hexagons 30-33, 73
Heydar Aliyev Center
    (Azerbaijan) 58
horizontal lines 90, 92, 93
hours 81, 82-83
human body 120-135
hundredths 88
hunger 122, 123

Ii

imperial units 22-23

Jj

Java 117
Jefferson, Thomas 109
jewellery 50-51

Ll

languages, coding 116, 117
length 22, 49, 129

less than 12
light 125
lines 57, 90
lines of symmetry 70
liquid 22-23, 68-69
location 95
loops, Möbius 66-67

Mm

maps 94-95, 109, 112-115
marble run 90-93
marshmallow shapes 28-29
materials 57
mean 130

measurement 22-23, 56,
    57, 106-107, 110-111,
    134-135
median 130
messages, secret 36-39
metric measurements
    22-23
midday 81, 124, 125
midnight 82
minarets 56
minus sign 13, 41

minutes 80
mirrors 70, 71
Mirzakhani, Maryam 27
Möbius loops 66-67
mode 131
money 41, 44-47, 89
months 83, 102, 103
more than 12
mosques 56-57
multiplication 24, 48-49,
    53, 69 74-75, 76-77,
    107
multiplication sign 48

Nn

natural symmetry 70-71
negative correlation 132
negative numbers 13
Neptune 94
nets, shape 60-65
Nishikado, Tomohiro
    118-119
number bonds 42-43
number lines 40-41

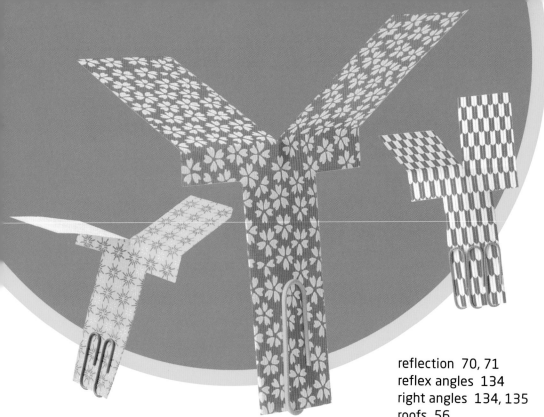

Oo

obtuse angles 134, 135
octagons 26
one, dividing by 53
one, multiplying by 48
one-dimensional
  surfaces 27
opposite operators 53
optical illusions 33
order of rotational
  symmetry 73
outliers 133
overlap segments 128-129

Pp

parallel lines 90, 92, 93
patterns 30-33, 104-105
pentagons 26
perimeter 107
perpendicular lines 90, 93
pets 128-129
pictograms 128-129
picture algorithm 96-97
pie charts 129
place value 13, 126-127
place-value columns 46-47
planets 94
plants 110-111

plotting co-ordinates 113,
  132
plus sign 40
Pluto 94
p.m. 81, 82, 123, 124, 125
politics 129
polygons 26
polymaths 108
Pont du Gard (France) 57
positive correlation
  132, 133
predictions 18
printing patterns 104-105
prism nets 64-65
prisms 29
probability 18-19
protractors 8, 122, 134,
  135
pyramids 29, 62

Qq

quarters 17

Rr

radius 96
rainfall 68-69
recipes 24-25
rectangles 26, 56, 107,
  134

reflection 70, 71
reflex angles 134
right angles 134, 135
roofs 56
rooms 106-107
rotational symmetry 72-73
rounding 106
routine 125
rows 74-75, 128

Ss

satellites 94-95
scales 20-21, 23
scatter graphs 110-111,
  132
scoring systems 118, 119
Second World War 36-37
seconds 80
seeds 110-111
sequences 104
shape nets 60-65
shapes 26-29, 56, 58-59
sharing 12, 52-53
shells 70, 71
shoe size 130, 131
shop, pretend 44-47
sides 26
six times table 49
sixteenths 17
slavery 109
sleep 122, 123, 125
smartphones 95
snack decider, spinning
  18-19
solar eclipses 109

space 94
Space Invaders 118-119
speed 86-87
spheres 27
spires 56
squared measurements 49, 106
squares 26, 56, 71, 107
stamps 104-105
starfish, rotating 72-73
statements, true or false 117
statistics 128-129, 130-131
stopwatches 89
subtracting 15, 40, 41, 46-47, 52
Sun 82, 83, 125
sunflowers 110-111
supercomputers 95, 116
surveying 109
symmetry 70-73

Tt

T-shirts 104-105
tablets 95

tallies 128, 131
tape measures 106
telescopes 109
temperatures 13, 23
tenths 88
tessellation 30-33
thermometers 23
thousandths 88
three-dimensional shapes 26, 27, 28-29, 60-65
time 23, 80-83, 87, 102-103, 108
times tables 49, 76-77
top score 119
treasure maps 112-115
triangles 26, 29, 56, 73, 134
triangular pyramids 29
true statements 117
two times table 49, 77
two-dimensional shapes 26

Vv

Venn diagrams 128-129
vertical lines 90, 93
vertices 27, 28
video games 116-119
volume 22-23, 68-69
voting 129

Ww

walls 106-107
Washington, D.C. 109
watches 108, 89
water 68-69
weather 94, 132
weeks 83
weight 20-21, 23, 84-85
West, Gladys 94-95
wheels 100-102
width 49, 69
wings 84

Xx

x-axis 110, 112-113, 132
x co-ordinates 113

Yy

y-axis 110, 112-113, 132
y co-ordinates 113
years 80, 83

Zz

zero, multiplying by 48

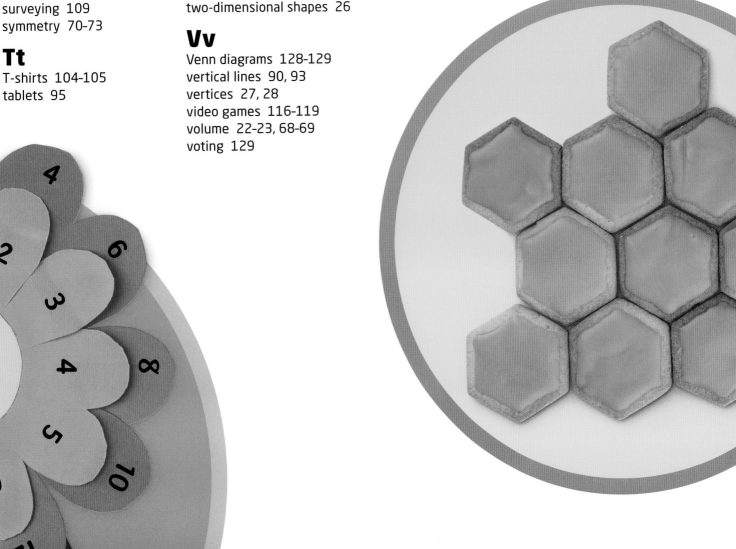

Acknowledgements

AMI would like to thank the Stemettes team for their patience while she worked on this book.
DK would like to thank the following: Polly Goodman for proofreading; Helen Peters for the index; and Eemeli Vuorhovi for his help with the computer coding spread.

The publisher would like to thank the following for their kind permission to reproduce their photographs:

(Key: a-above; b-below/bottom; c-centre; f-far; l-left; r-right; t-top)

4 Dreamstime.com: Liubov Shirokova (br). **8 Dreamstime.com:** Exopixel (bl). **13 Dreamstime.com:** Mariusz Blach (l); Kostyantine Pankin (crb). **16 Dorling Kindersley:** Rotring UK Ltd (tr). **18 Dorling Kindersley:** Rotring UK Ltd (tc). **19 123RF.com:** pixelrobot (cra). **20 123RF.com:** Anton Starikov (tl). **23 Dreamstime.com:** Laralova (bl). **Getty Images:** Sharon Vos-Arnold (clb). **27 123RF.com:** Aleksanderdn (bl). **Alamy Stock Photo:** Epa European Pressphoto Agency B.V. (tr). **31 Dreamstime.com:** Piotr Pawinski / Ppart (tr). **33 Dreamstime.com:** Waclawmostowski (tr). **34-35 Dreamstime.com:** Icefront. **37 Dorling Kindersley:** Imperial War Museum, London (tr). **40 Dreamstime.com:** Mikhail Kokhanchikov (tl). **iStockphoto.com:** FatCamera (cb). **41 Alamy Stock Photo:** Sergey Novikov (cb, clb). **Dreamstime.com:** Mikhail Kokhanchikov (t). **44 Dorling Kindersley:** Rotring UK Ltd (tc). **44-45 123RF.com:** Ekaterina Bychkova (b). **45 123RF.com:** Ekaterina Bychkova (c); Hugo Lacasse (c/yellow). **46-47 123RF.com:** Ekaterina Bychkova (c). **47 123RF.com:** Alexmit (ca). **48 Dreamstime.com:** Inkaphotoimage (cr). **49 Dorling Kindersley:** Jerry Young (tc). **Dreamstime.com:** Stefan Hermans / Perrush (tl). **50 Dreamstime.com:** Piotr Pawinski / Ppart (tr). **52 123RF.com:** Alexmit (ca). **Dreamstime.com:** Aldo Di Bari Murga / Aldodi (ca/Baseball). **53 123RF.com:** Alexmit (cl). **Dreamstime.com:** Aldo Di Bari Murga / Aldodi (ca); Costasz (tc). **54-55 Dreamstime.com:** La Fabrika Pixel S.I. **56 Alamy Stock Photo:** Imagenet (b). **57 Alamy Stock Photo:** Jimmy Villalta / VWPics (tr). **Dreamstime.com:** Alessandroguerriero (cr); Martinmolcan (tl); Filip Fuxa (cla); Milanmarkovic (bc). **58-59 Alamy Stock Photo:** Elnur Amikishiyev (b). **59 Alamy Stock Photo:** Arcaid Images (c). **70 123RF.com:** Liubov Shirokova (fcr). **71 Dreamstime.com:** Sofiaworld (fcl). **74 Alamy Stock Photo:** Paul Doyle (crb).

Dreamstime.com: Photka (tc). **78-79 123RF.com:** Teerachat Aebwanawong. **80 Dorling Kindersley:** Steve Lyne (tc). **Dreamstime.com:** Svetlana Foote / Saddako123 (fcla). **81 123RF.com:** Brian Kinney (tr). **82 Dreamstime.com:** Kidsada Manchinda (cla). **83 Dreamstime.com:** Photka (crb). **84 Dreamstime.com:** Ilya Genkin / Igenkin (b). **89 123RF.com:** Olga Solovieva (cla). **Dreamstime.com:** Newlight (bl). **94 Getty Images:** Erik Simonsen (bl). **95 123RF.com:** Georgejmclittle (tl). **96 Dorling Kindersley:** Rotring UK Ltd (tc). **100-101 Dreamstime.com:** Judgar. **103 Dorling Kindersley:** Stephen Oliver (tc). **109 123RF.com:** Solarseven (tl). **Alamy Stock Photo:** FLHC 96 (cr); Science History Images (bc). **110 Dreamstime.com:** Dijarm (l). **111 Dreamstime.com:** Dijarm (bl); Firina (r). **112 Dorling Kindersley:** Rotring UK Ltd (tr). **117 Alamy Stock Photo:** Thomas Imo (bl). **118 Alamy Stock Photo:** Mark Murphy (clb). **119 Dreamstime.com:** Radistmorze (crb). **Getty Images:** Lluis Gene / AFP (tr). **120-121 123RF.com:** belchonock. **122 Dorling Kindersley:** Rotring UK Ltd (tr). **Dreamstime.com:** Exopixel

(cla, tc). **123 Dorling Kindersley:** Stephen Oliver (tc). **124 123RF.com:** rawpixel (c). **Depositphotos Inc:** Helen_F (ca). **125 Dreamstime.com:** Frenta (c); Ramona Kaulitzki (c/Moon and stars). **128 123RF.com:** Marigranula (crb). **128-129 Fotolia:** Eric Isselee (cb). **129 123RF.com:** Marigranula (ca). **Alamy Stock Photo:** Stephen Barnes / Politics (br). **Fotolia:** Eric Isselee (cla). **132 Dreamstime.com:** Dijarm (tl). **133 Dreamstime.com:** Dijarm (b). **134 Dreamstime.com:** Torsakarin (tc). **135 Dreamstime.com:** Jose Manuel Gelpi Diaz (tr). **136 Dreamstime.com:** Ken Cole (bl); Monkey Business Images / Monkeybusinessimages (clb); Ion Adrian Popa (r). **Getty Images:** Stocktrek Images (clb/storm). **NASA:** Tony Gray and Tom Farrar (cl). **140 Dorling Kindersley:** Imperial War Museum, London (bl)

Cover images: *Front:* **Paparazzi VIP / Anne-Marie Imafidon:** tr

All other images © Dorling Kindersley
For further information see:
www.dkimages.com

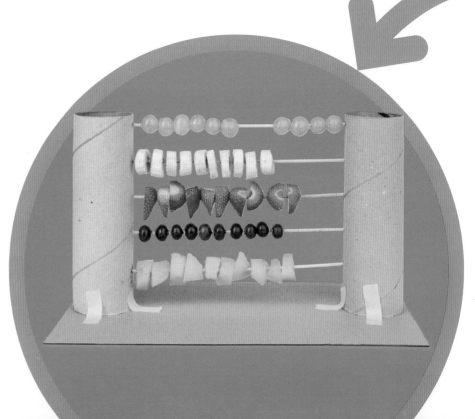